PENGUIN BOOKS
COMICS TO CLASSICS

Arthea J. S. Reed is called "Charlie" by her students, family, and friends. She lives in Asheville, North Carolina, in the beautiful Blue Ridge Mountains, with Donald, her husband, and two dogs. She has taught in middle schools and high schools in three states, and she spends a great deal of time with her two teenaged nieces.

For the last sixteen years, Charlie has taught at the University of North Carolina at Asheville. She is currently professor and chair of the education department. She is the author of *Reaching Adolescents: The Young Adult Book and the School* and for six years was the editor of *The ALAN Review*, one of the most highly regarded and recognized journals in the field of young adult literature. She is the co-editor of the Penguin/Signet Classic teachers' guide series, in which authors include young adult books to use as bridges to the classical works. She teaches courses in adolescent literature to pre-service teachers, in-service teachers, librarians, and parents. She lectures widely in the field of young adult literature and on the topic of censorship.

With her co-author Verna E. Bergemann, Charlie is currently revising two textbooks designed for foundation or introductory education courses. *In the Classroom: An Introduction to Education* and *Observation and Participation in the Classroom* were both published in 1992, with second editions scheduled to appear in 1995.

Charlie is also the current chair of the National Council of Teachers of English (eighth grade) Promising Young Writers competition. She has served on numerous local and state commissions dealing with issues related to children and to education and has published articles in a variety of journals.

COMICS

TO

CLASSICS

. . . .

A Guide to Books for
Teens and Preteens

ARTHEA J. S. REED

Foreword by Jim Trelease

PENGUIN BOOKS

PENGUIN BOOKS
Published by the Penguin Group
Penguin Books USA Inc., 375 Hudson Street,
New York, New York 10014, U.S.A.
Penguin Books Ltd, 27 Wrights Lane, London W8 5TZ, England
Penguin Books Australia Ltd, Ringwood, Victoria, Australia
Penguin Books Canada Ltd, 10 Alcorn Avenue,
Toronto, Ontario, Canada M4V 3B2
Penguin Books (N.Z.) Ltd, 182–190 Wairau Road,
Auckland 10, New Zealand

Penguin Books Ltd, Registered Offices:
Harmondsworth, Middlesex, England

First published in the United States of America by
International Reading Association 1988
This updated and revised edition published in Penguin Books 1994

10 9 8 7 6 5 4 3 2 1

Grateful acknowledgment is made for permission to reprint "The Fervent Prayer of
a Teenager's Parent," by Richard Peck. By permission of the author.

LIBRARY OF CONGRESS CATALOGING IN PUBLICATION DATA
Reed, Arthea J. S.
Comics to classics: a guide to books for teens and preteens/
Arthea J. S. Reed.
p. cm.
Previously published: Newark, Del.: International Reading
Association, © 1988.
Includes bibliographical references.
ISBN 0 14 02.3712 7
1. Teenagers—United States—Books and reading. 2. Children—
United States—Books and reading. 3. Reading—Parent
participation—United States. 4. Young adult literature—
Bibliography. 5. Children's literature—Bibliography. I. Title.
Z1037.A1R428 1994
028.1'6250835—dc20   94–5094

Printed in the United States of America
Set in Cheltenham Light Condensed
Designed by Ann Gold

TO STEPHANIE AND JENNIFER

Foreword

Talking with a group of parents one day, the great child psychologist Bruno Bettelheim tried to put the momentousness of their parenting into perspective. He told them, "For the rest of your life you will never be as important to anyone else as you are to your child today."

If you doubt that, consider the following:

- When she discovered her child was the worst reader in his Detroit fifth-grade class, Sonia Carson limited him to two hours of television a week and required him to give her book reports on two books a week. The reports had to be oral, because the mother's own reading wasn't that strong with just a third-grade education. Today her son is the preeminent pediatric brain surgeon in America.

- When all the other Lutheran boys received a watch and a pair of long pants for confirmation, Mrs. Von Braun gave her son Werner a telescope instead.

- There was a rule in the luxurious Eisner home overlooking New York's Central Park: If son Michael wanted to watch television, that was fine—as long as he read two hours for every one hour of watching. Today that son is the CEO of Disney.

- Mrs. Shaw was a domestic and Mr. Shaw was a house painter, which left them little money for luxuries. But reading was considered a necessity, and there were four daily newspapers in the home and subscriptions to two black weeklies. Today their son Bernard is a CNN anchorman.

- Anne Hamill landed in New York from Belfast, Northern Ireland, on the day the stock market crashed in 1929 and she lived for years as an indentured servant. Eventually she married, began a family, and worked as a movie theater cashier. Among her rules: Her children were not allowed into the theater until each had a library card and could read. Today her children include an engineer, an editor for Navy publications, a photographer, a television producer, and three writers—one of whom is Pete Hamill, the columnist and novelist.

- Clara sensed that reading to her daughter was the right thing to do, even before the child could read herself. But she mistakenly believed that if children read on their own before the age of eight, it would damage their eyes and minds. The four-year-old, however, was so taken with the stories her mother read to her and the little mystery tales she told that she incessantly pestered the adults around her to explain signs and words until she taught herself to read before age five—much to her mother's dismay. Little did she know, of course, that the child she initiated into the world of books would grow up to become Agatha Christie—who still had both her eyesight and mind intact well into her eighties.

Just by holding this book in your hands, chances are that you, like the above-mentioned parents, are interested in or concerned about your child as a reader. Welcome to the club.

While membership in this "club" is informal and open to anyone, it is somewhat "exclusive." Exclusive in the unfortunate sense that potential members—that is, parents—keep excluding themselves, opting instead to join shopping clubs, health clubs, television clubs, and video clubs. Reading, they mistakenly guess, would take too much time and energy. "And besides, my kid's reading is the business of his teacher. As a parent, what do I know about reading?"

That depends on how much you *want* to know. If you read this book, you'll know a lot more about children and their reading than you knew before.

You are a member of the largest and most important teacher corps in the world—you are a parent. Everything that keeps us civilized, everything that is truly important, is taught us by our parents: how to live, how to love, and even how to work. This is accomplished largely through example and imitation. Or, as my Irish grandmother used to say, "The apple doesn't fall far from the tree."

For more reasons than biological, I am a parent because my parents were. As a child, I liked what I saw happening in my home and decided to do likewise in my own home. I am a reader for the same reason. I saw and heard my parents reading every day. Must be important, I thought, and so I began my life as a reader. Although occasional exceptions do surface, it's safe to say that readers raise readers.

For the moment, let's assume you have done all the right things up to this point: Your child has seen and heard you reading; there are books, magazines, and newspapers in the home; and everyone in the family owns a library card. We might even safely say your child enjoys reading. As his or her appetite, hair, skin, voice, clothes, friends, and taste in music begin to suffer dramatic changes, you are worried that the child's reading appetite will change. Rest assured it will. But *you* have much to do with whether it changes for the better or worse.

If you haven't replaced the books your child read in fifth grade, if your weekly trip to the library has become a monthly one, and if you find the family returning more borrowed videos than borrowed books, please note that these are warning signs, signaling a "dangerous curve" in reading.

Keep in mind that reading—like riding a bicycle—is an acquired skill. The more you read, the better you read; and the better you read, the more you like reading. Conversely, the less you read, the less you enjoy reading. Therefore the trick is to keep a child reading through adolescence.

As the earlier parent anecdotes exemplify, the environment you create or promote in your home is essential. Is television viewing limited? Is there a reading lamp beside your child's bed? Do you include magazine subscriptions and books among the gifts you give your teen? Is there a plentiful supply of reading material in the family room, bedroom, bathroom, and kitchen? Most important, do you lead by example? Does your child see you reading? And if so, what do you read?

One of the best things you can do to raise a reader through adolescence is to read adolescent literature. If you have never read teen or preteen literature, it will both surprise and please you—and some of it will challenge and even *provoke* you. But until you have read adolescent literature, you will never be able to enthuse over it or discuss it. Your child may then figure you don't care, and if *you're* not interested, why should he or she be?

Arthea (Charlie) Reed's compilation of titles and annotations is a wonderful guide through the forest of young adult literature, not just for parents but for everyone who cares about teens— aunts, uncles, coaches, librarians, teachers, and, obviously, students themselves.

Most of us know the books teenagers hate. Some of us still

have scar tissue from when they were forced down our throats in junior and senior high school—the books that seemed to specialize in turning readers *off* instead of turning them *on*. (I suspect there were English department chairs who mistakenly rationalized: Since reading dies in most people by age nineteen, we'd better squeeze in Shakespeare and Hardy before it's too late. Didn't they ever wonder *why* reading died?) In any case, you'll find none of those books here. Instead, here are the books that keep young readers reading, thinking, enjoying, and sharing with one another.

Professor Neil Postman once observed, "Children are the living messages we send to a time we will never see." Consider the messages sent by the parents at the start of this essay to be packages of values handed from parent to child. And now weigh the messages you are sending.

—Jim Trelease
author of *The New Read-Aloud Handbook*

Preface

Ah, adolescence! If you are like most parents, adolescence is a time in your child's life that you have anxiously awaited with equal amounts of optimism and despair. You remember the problems and frustrations of your own adolescence. You have heard from the media and friends and have read in books and magazines about how difficult it is to be an adolescent and to be the parent of an adolescent. You worry about cars and drugs and sex and disease. You are concerned whether you will be able to talk to your adolescent child or will be cut off as he or she discovers new interests and finds new friends.

It is equally likely that you have anticipated your child's adolescence with excitement. For you and for your adolescent, it is a time of increased mobility and freedom. You remember your own carefree adolescence—the delightful days of school, athletic events, dates, and endless phone conversations. During your adolescence you met your parents as real people for the first time, and you anticipate numerous adult conversations with your adolescent child. For parents and for the young, adolescence is indeed a time, as Norma Fox Mazer describes it, of "energy, enthusiasm, confusion, hope, despair, love, optimism, faith, and belief."

I will not attempt to gloss over the problems of adolescence, nor will I offer solutions to all of the difficulties that lie ahead for you and the adolescent you love. I will provide you, however, with information about what you can expect of your adolescent as she or he grows and develops. My philosophy, based on many years of experience, is that reading helps adolescents reduce the stress of their confused lives as they discover that others face similar difficulties and experience similar despair. I will discuss at length books appropriate for a variety of adolescent readers. In the pages ahead you will discover ways to encourage your adolescent to read, methods for selecting books for your adolescent, techniques for making television and films a positive influence on your adolescent, and ideas for keeping the lines of communication open between the two of you. There is no doubt that adolescence can be difficult. However, it can also be a time of great optimism, love, enthusiasm, and faith shared by you and your adolescent child. Through books, reading, and discussion you and the adolescent can turn the difficulties and despair of adolescence into positive contributions toward an optimistic, healthy adult life.

Acknowledgments

Writing a book requires the work of many individuals without whom the book would never be published. First and foremost, thanks go to my students, who have taught me much of what I know about adolescents and adolescent literature. The middle and high school students who first passed on to me their enthusiasm for adolescent literature deserve special thanks. The students in my adolescent literature classes at the University of North Carolina at Asheville continue to introduce me to new books and authors that they, their adolescent children, and their students have come to love. Thanks go to the student assistants in the office of the UNCA Department of Education who helped type the manuscript, run errands, and do research: Lara Koerber, Karen Shelton, Michelle Fox, and especially Lyn Clarkson, who was able to find information that no one else could.

The experiences of numerous parents and their children fill the pages of this book. Without them the story could not be told. They have provided me with new insights and a renewed respect for the power of books and of positive parenting.

Of course, this book could not have been written if it were not for the wonderful writers of books for adolescents. Not only are these individuals gifted writers, but they care deeply about their readers. Thank you for letting me share your books and thoughts on adolescence, books for adolescents, and the writing process. Your words enliven the pages of this book and make reading a joy for millions of young people. Thanks, too, to the publishers who publish books for adolescents and who sent them to me for review and possible inclusion in this book.

Without my trusted and talented assistant Judy Carver, this book and much of my other work would never be completed. She keeps the office running smoothly while I am absorbed in the writing process. Also, thanks to the helpful staff at Ramsey Library who never hesitate to look up a bibliographic reference, locate an address, or search for obscure information. Particular thanks go to Nancy Hayes.

Every book needs a good editor. Thanks go to Caroline White, who has seen this project through to completion. Special thanks to Dan Lundy, who had faith in me and in this book.

It is difficult to imagine how any book could be completed without a supportive spouse. My husband, Don, supported me intellectually and emotionally as I struggled to complete the book. He read each chapter numerous times; he gently made suggestions for changes. And he kept the household running when I was too busy to think about cooking or cleaning. Without his support, this project would have been impossible.

And finally, thanks to our teenage nieces, Stephanie and Jennifer, who read books for me and with me, always giving me their honest opinions. The discussions we have had about books have enlivened our relationships and provided me with the opportunity to test my ideas about books in general and about discussing books and reading them aloud in particular.

Contents

ONE

. . . .

Teens and Preteens

1

. . . .

The Preadolescent and Reading

The land of the young is the land of energy, enthusiasm, confusion, hope, despair, love, optimism, faith, and belief.

Norma Fox Mazer

The Preadolescent

Preadolescence is a time when a child is no longer a child but not yet an adult. It is an in-between, difficult time that is hard to define in terms of age. Maturation begins at different ages and continues at rates that vary from individual to individual.

A seventh-grade classroom is a good place to observe the differences in physical, social, emotional, and intellectual maturity in young people who are about the same age. Jennifer, who is 12.5 years old, is physically mature but acts like a child. Sean, at four feet seven inches and almost thirteen years old, answers questions with the maturity of an adult. Barbara, 12.4 years, not only looks mature but acts mature, at least socially. She spends an entire class period making eyes at Ramon. Ramon, 12.8 years, also is physically mature, but, unlike Barbara, he has no interest in the opposite sex. He has the latest copy of *Sports Illustrated* in his desk and reads it whenever he gets a chance. Who are these young people? How will they change in the next few years? What are their reading interests today? What will they read next year and the year after?

All of these young people are adolescents. Some are in the midst of puberty; others have not left childhood. For all of them, it is a time of physical change and intense involvement with peers.

Physical Development and Attachment to Peers

By late childhood (ages 10–13), children are experiencing significant physical change. Psychologist Robert Havighurst explains that this change can cause hyperactivity, rebelliousness, moodiness, and irritability, and it can diminish self-confidence just when preadolescents are striving to build it.

One of my favorite pastimes is watching young people at a local swimming pool. Since I see many of these young people only at the pool, the physical changes I observe when the pool opens in June can be startling. Consider a group of girls I watched recently. The summer before, they had been children who were constantly active, jumping out of the pool, climbing the ladder, and jumping off the high dive. Their legs were skinny and their chests were flat. In one year incredible physical and social changes had occurred. All but one had grown several inches and all were beginning to look like young women.

Their behavior had changed too. No longer did they shout across the pool to their mothers. Now they wanted to be seen only with their peers. Two of the girls arrived at the pool carrying large boom boxes. They all had nearly identical beach bags stocked with coconut oil, brushes, and beach towels. They found several lounge chairs directly across from the lifeguard and set up shop. I observed them for nearly two hours, and not one of them got wet.

I was not sure of the girls' ages, but they appeared to be about twelve. Like most young people that age, they rarely sat still. Though their towels remained on the chairs, the girls were on the move. In two hours I counted three trips to the soda machine, four walks around the perimeter of the pool, two trips to the water fountain, countless trips to the restroom, and two trips to the telephone. None of the girls traveled alone.

The physical differences in the girls' maturation clearly influenced their self-confidence. One of them had developed far more than her peers, and she obviously found this embarrassing. Every time she got up to visit friends or to run to the soda machine, she put an oversized shirt over her bathing suit. Another girl had matured little since the previous summer; she sat with a towel draped around her one-piece suit.

The girls' interactions with their mothers also had changed. Late in the afternoon, one of the mothers came to pick them up. The previous year they had darted repeatedly from the pool to Mother's beach chair; now they practically ignored her. She walked over to their chairs, said a few words to them (which they tried to ignore), moved away to talk to a friend, and finally began calling to them impatiently. As they slowly packed their gear, they never acknowledged her presence.

Change Affects Both Sexes

Boys, too, find it difficult to deal with the physical changes of adolescence. Rapid growth can make it almost impossible for boys to sit still, so they often appear to be hyperactive and clumsy. These traits make it difficult for boys to function in a cramped classroom. At the same time, preadolescents are attempting to pull away from adult authority. Consequently, boys frequently instigate classroom disturbances that call attention to themselves, defy classroom rules, and annoy the teacher.

Boys, like girls, are frequently embarrassed by physical changes. A friend of mine told me about her eleven-year-old son's first day at school this fall. Danny came to the breakfast table asking his mother for a bar of soap; he had discovered his first pimple. His mother chuckled that there are some advantages to adolescence; this was the first time Danny had worried about his personal appearance and associated it with good hygiene. Probably the most humiliating change for young men is voice change, which usually occurs during the preadolescent years. Jeff Garrett, a character in Lois Duncan's *Killing Mr. Griffin*, recalls the embarrassment (p. 24).

> Jeff had been twelve then, big for his age, standing head and shoulders above the others in the seventh-grade classroom. He had felt huge and self-conscious. His voice had already been starting to change. When roll was called he answered with a froglike croak, and the rest of the class had burst into laughter.
>
> Even the teacher had smiled, and Jeff had felt the sting of hot tears in his eyes. He had blinked them back, furious at himself, hating all of them. Choking on his own fury, he had wedged himself into the seat behind the desk, wishing he could disappear beneath it.

・ ・ ・ ・ ・ ・

The Preadolescent Reader

According to G. Robert Carlsen, a well-known scholar in the field of literature for young adults, the peak of reading interest occurs around age twelve. By then most preadolescents can read comfortably a wide range of materials on a variety of reading levels. When young readers enter middle or junior high school, they are no longer learning to read in the sense of learning to gain basic meaning from the written word. Instead, they are "reading to learn."

Expanding Interests

By the time preadolescents are twelve, their interests have expanded beyond the neighborhood and school. They are curious about many things. However, they have limited capabilities for exploring their widening world. Most preadolescents are limited by how far they can walk or pedal, how far the bus or subway goes, or how far their parents are willing to drive them. Most have limited funds and are restricted by parental regulations; few have jobs outside of the home or neighborhood. Much of their interest and curiosity must be satisfied by television, movies, and books.

Donald Gallo, in a study of the reading interests of students in grades four through twelve, found that only 6 percent of all students classified themselves as nonreaders, whereas 20 percent called themselves avid readers. The average student in his survey claimed to read between three and five hours per week independently. Thirty-nine percent of all preadolescents reported reading three or four books outside of school per month, whereas most of the students (87 percent) at all grade levels reported reading at least one book per month independently.

Gallo's study found a wide range of reading interests. For preadolescent girls, whom he found to be more avid readers than boys, books dealing with problems of growing up were most popular, followed by books about animals, mystery/suspense, and romance/love. Sports was the most popular topic of books for preadolescent boys. A distant second, according to Gallo, was science fiction, followed by horror/supernatural, adventure/survival, and mystery/suspense.

How Reading Skills Develop

Reading is a skill that develops slowly. It is probably true that some people have a natural ability that makes it easier for them to read. Likewise, some people grow up in environments that allow them to develop reading skills with ease and enjoyment.

These environments are filled with books and have adults who read independently as well as read to their children. It is also true that most young people are capable of learning to read. Bruno Bettelheim and Karen Zelan say that if young readers are allowed to develop reading skills naturally, in supportive environments, and without undue pressure, they are likely to become readers by the time they leave elementary school.

Like most other skills, reading develops in stages. Educator Margaret Early explains that the earliest stage of reading development begins long before children can identify letters or words. She calls this period the stage of "unconscious enjoyment," which begins during the preschool years and continues until preadolescence. During this time, children love to play with words, to hear words repeated, to make rhymes and riddles, to sing, and to create nonsense words and sentences. According to Early, this love of language and the ability to play with words fortifies children as they struggle to learn to read. Children who have not discovered the joy of language may experience difficulty in learning to read, since learning to read requires playing with language and trying out new sounds, techniques, and words. Parents should encourage this playfulness in their preadolescent children. The fun young readers have with reading will allow them to develop normally through the other stages of reading development. (See the chart on page 9 and chapters 2 and 3 for more information on this and later stages of reading development.)

Reading Progress

The National Assessment of Educational Progress (NAEP) is a program that tests and surveys nine-, thirteen-, and seventeen-year-old students in the United States to determine their educational progress. Since 1971 reading test scores have risen significantly for African American and Hispanic students and shown limited improvement for white students, although white students still out-

DEVELOPMENTAL READING STAGES

Estimated Beginning Age	*Stage Marked by:*
3–5 years of age	(1) Unconscious enjoyment of language and books (fortifies child's learning to decode)
10–14 years of age	(2) Egocentric interest in reading and books (exerts some effort to enhance delight in books; wants to become part of the story; story must be believable)
17+ years of age	(3) Aesthetic interest in reading and books (exercises discriminating judgment; deeper feeling for mankind replaces concern for self)

NOTES:

(a) Reader does not abandon one stage when entering another.

(b) Most secondary school students are at stage 2 and have an egocentric interest in books.

(c) Most readers do not reach stage 3.

(d) Most readers must progress through the stages in order; it is unusual for a reader to skip a stage.

Based on: Margaret Early, *Stages in Growth in Literary Appreciation*, 1960, 161–67.

score both African American and Hispanic students. Recent tests indicate that virtually all thirteen-year-olds (94 percent) read with basic skills and understanding, while more than half (59 percent) can interrelate ideas and make generalizations while they read. Although virtually no thirteen-year-olds read at the most advanced, adult levels, 11 percent are adept readers who can understand complicated information.

For parents the most interesting aspect of the NAEP program

is the information revealed in a comparison of student surveys and test scores. Two items seem to affect reading test scores the most: amount of time spent doing homework and the amount of time spent reading independently each day. According to the survey/test comparisons, students who spend more time doing homework and more time reading independently read better than students who spend less time on homework and reading. Therefore, if preadolescents are to develop advanced, adult reading skills, it is essential that parents monitor the completion of assigned homework and encourage independent reading.

This period of transition from childhood to young adulthood can be trying for preadolescents and their parents. However, if their homes provide a comfortable place of refuge, preadolescents are likely to continue to look upon the family as a source of comfort and protection while seeking new roles in their ever-expanding world. If we, as parents, help our youngsters capitalize on the energy, enthusiasm, hope, love, optimism, faith, and belief of youth and minimize their confusion and despair, they should pass through these years with relative ease.

Likewise, if parents remain or become involved with the education of their preadolescents by monitoring their homework and requiring that it be completed, the students will become more proficient readers. Independent reading is also essential if preadolescents are to learn to read at more advanced levels. Parents should encourage their children to select books that are likely to be of interest to them and make it possible for them to read these books daily.

2

. . . .

The Early Adolescent and Reading

During adolescence we encounter the most deeply felt things in life —love, fear of rejection, death perhaps, and intense happiness. We often respond with greater emotion than at any other point in our lives. Adolescence is often a worrisome period of pressures— pressure to do well in school, to gain acceptance from friends, to cope with problems without the benefit of experience that adults often take for granted.

Kevin Major

The Early Adolescent

Early adolescence, between the ages of thirteen and fifteen, is marked by rapid growth and physical development. Youngsters in this group are often restless and rebellious. According to Margaret A. Edwards, author of *The Fair Garden and the Swarm of Beasts: The Library and the Young Adult*, "The adolescent is bound by confusion and bewilderment in his attempts to find out who he is and what identity to assume. He needs to know others who have been under the same constraints and have freed themselves. . . . As he matures, the young person wants to break out of his shell and become involved with others. He wants to be free from the narrow confines of self and find meaning for his life." Early adolescents establish relationships with peers, first of the same sex and later of the opposite sex. In addition, they begin to seek their own identity within the conformity of the peer group. This causes potential for conflict between peers and family and can result in personal identity problems and changed relationships with parents.

Peer Group and Family: A Potential Conflict

Even while conforming to the peer group, early adolescents begin to seek a personal identity. It is not unusual to hear junior high or early high school students say "I want to be accepted for who I am." But "who I am" is often dictated by the peer group. This is a potential conflict for early adolescents.

Early adolescents also begin to establish new relationships at home. They want increased freedom from parents and rules. They are likely to develop opinions that reflect those of the peer group and express them freely. Early adolescents may change the way they dress and seek more freedom to decide with whom to spend time and when, where, and how often. They start looking for new ways of getting money, recognizing that money leads to increased independence. This pull away from the family can lead to conflict, and unresolved conflict can lead to rebellion.

On the other hand, early adolescents often fear their new independence and seek support from the family. They may fight against rules, but they often find constraints comforting. Stephanie, who is fourteen, argues frequently with her parents about being allowed to go places with her peers. However, she also reports that she is glad she has to be home at 11:00 P.M. so that she doesn't have to spend more time with "that dork." Her slang term for her date may simply mean she does not like him, or it may mean that he is involved in activities that she is relieved to avoid.

We do not know why some early adolescents have little difficulty progressing through the early adolescent years, while others are overwhelmed by conflicting goals and values. We do know, however, that early adolescents must establish new relationships with peers and family and at the same time establish a new identity for themselves. Psychologist Abraham Maslow refers to the adolescent's conflict between parents and peer group as the tension of developing needs. The early adolescent is struggling to meet the need for safety (security; stability; dependency; protection; freedom from fear, anxiety, and chaos; need for structure, order, law, limits; strength in the protector; and so on) provided by parents and other adults. He or she is also seeking to meet the need for social affection (belongingness or love) provided by the peer group. When the structure and order of the family seem to get in the way of the adolescent's acceptance by the peer group, conflict may develop.

Developing Values of the Early Adolescent

Understanding how adolescents develop moral reasoning and values may help explain why some young teens find the conflict between the home and the peer group unsolvable. It is important for parents to recognize that the values of early adolescents are determined by values and rules set by parents and other adults in authority. According to psychologist Lawrence Kohlberg, most early adolescents who are developing normally are at the stage he calls conventional moral reasoning at which they comply with rules based on the expectation of reward. They base their judgments on the approval of family, traditional values, laws of society, and loyalty to country. At an earlier stage of values development, preconventional moral reasoning, younger children's behaviors are predicated on the concrete approval of others. At the conventional stage moral behavior is based on law and authority in the desire to avoid guilt and censure. Therefore, developmentally appropriate rules, based on the values that the adolescent has been taught, are exceedingly important to early adolescents. If the adolescent does not have the security of these rules, he or she is likely to abide by the "rules" established by the peer group. Frequently these rules are in conflict with mature, adult moral values. On the other hand, if the rules by which the adolescent must abide are not compatible with his or her intellectual, psychological, and emotional development, he or she may feel compelled to rebel against those rules. For example, Stephanie's parents have provided her with a curfew that fits in with their expectations of her at home and at school. They have also limited her access to some social events that they believe are above her maturity level. However, they encourage her to choose between a variety of age-appropriate activities and often allow her to decide whether or not she will participate in family events. This summer she wanted to attend a French camp that was in session at the same time as a family camping vacation. Although her parents would have preferred to have her along on the family trip, they allowed her to make the decision and she went to the French camp.

• • • • • •

The Egocentric Early Adolescent Reader

By the time they are early adolescents, youngsters have progressed to what Margaret Early (see chart in chapter 1, p. 9) refers to as the egocentric stage of reading development. This stage corresponds with the adolescent's struggle for peer acceptance and personal identity. Even in selecting reading material, early adolescents seek to meet these egocentric needs.

This egocentric interest can be seen in the books selected by early adolescents. In his survey of adolescent reading interest, Donald Gallo found that 57 percent of early adolescent girls picked romance/love as their favorite topic of books to read for pleasure. Mystery/suspense was a distant second, followed by problems of growing up, horror/supernatural, fantasy, true stories, animals, cartoons/humor, adventure/survival, famous classics, sexuality, and family life. Boys overwhelmingly (47 percent) selected sports as their favorite topic of books. In a distant second place was science fiction, followed closely by horror/supernatural, adventure/survival, and mystery/suspense. Way down the list in terms of popularity came war, cartoons/humor, fantasy, true stories, animals, and history.

Becoming a Reader

By late junior high or early senior high school, teenagers can read independently and are willing to exert some effort on reading. However, if reading a book requires too much effort, readers are likely to become frustrated and quit reading it. If they are frustrated too often, they may quit reading altogether. This is understandable when we consider that early adolescents need to be in control of their own lives. If books consistently defeat youngsters and make them feel inferior, they are likely to quit reading. It is less embarrassing to quit reading than to feel inadequate.

Parents must be aware of this problem. Many parents would like their children to read the classics, but most early adolescents are neither emotionally nor intellectually mature enough to meet the demands of these books. If we force books on our children, again they may quit reading entirely. However, if we help them find appropriate books, they are likely to become avid readers who will continue to select books based on their increasing emotional and intellectual maturity.

Establishing an Identity through Books

Adolescents can use books to help establish their own identities. According to Early, it is important for early adolescent readers to see themselves in the characters, plots, and themes of the books they read. If readers find stories unbelievable, characters unrealistic, or themes obscure, they are likely to call the book "boring" or "dumb" and to discard it. If they do continue reading (perhaps because the book is required), they will do so with resentment. Herein lies another danger. Youngsters who frequently read books that do not meet their egocentric needs may decide that all books are a waste of time. Therefore, when we suggest books to early adolescents, we should seek books with young characters who deal with the realistic concerns of adolescents.

Characters Must Live Adolescence

Able readers at this stage of development also face another danger. Adults enjoy nostalgic books about adolescence that feature a central character who looks at these years in retrospect. Adolescents, however, are living their youth. Many retrospective books appear to young readers to speak down to them and to preach. Adolescents are put off by these books, in spite of the fact that the characters are young. Parents cannot assume that because a book has a young character it is appropriate for young egocentric readers. Characters must be living through adolescence, not looking back on it.

Parents Can Provide Guidance

It is during the stage of egocentric reading development that parents can provide significant help and guidance. Without the support of parents, adolescents frequently quit reading. The books adolescents are required to read in school rarely relate to their needs and interests; they reflect the world of adult literature. Consequently, it is especially important that books they read for pleasure meet their needs for peer acceptance and the establishment of a personal identity.

Likewise, the books early adolescents select often are not appropriate for their increasing maturity. For example, the romance/love novels most read by early adolescent girls fall into the publishing category of formula and series books. Series like "Sweet Valley High" may be appropriate for thirteen-year-olds but are likely to be too predictable and boring to fifteen-year-olds. However, often these youngsters do not know how to find other romance books that will appeal to their increasing maturity. Unfortunately, many of these young readers begin reading adult romances that do not meet their developmental needs. It is important for parents to help adolescent girls find more mature young adult romances with young characters to whom the adolescent can relate. These books as well as more mature sports books for early adolescent males are suggested in chapter 11. Parents who know their adolescent children and who are acquainted with young adult literature—literature written for and read by adolescents aged ten to eighteen—can introduce their youngsters to books that will meet their needs and help them become mature adult readers.

Early adolescence is a period of potential conflict both within the adolescent and between adolescents and adults. It is also an exciting time in which the restless energy of the teenager can be put to positive use. It is a time in which adolescents are willing to exert effort not only in the area of reading, but in the areas of personal development, interpersonal relationships, and social problems. Many young people grow into thinking, caring young adults during this period. Though parents may feel they have little influence on their teenagers, the examples they provide, th they set, and the understanding they exhibit allow their relationships with their adolescents to mature. Parents who help their adolescent children find realistic books with real characters are likely to help these young people develop into mature and capable readers.

3

The Late Adolescent and Reading

I want to give you a glimpse of the choices you have before you, of the price that will be asked of you. . . . When you know what life has to sell, for how much, and what it can give away free, you will not live in darkness. I hope that in books you'll find your light, and that by this light you may cross from one shore of love to another, from your childhood into adulthood.

Maia Wojciechowska, speaking to adolescent readers

The Late Adolescent

The late adolescent, between the ages of fifteen and eighteen, looks like an adult and wants to be treated as an adult, but lacks the experience, wisdom, and maturity of adulthood. Growth slows down during this period. Most girls of sixteen and boys of eighteen have reached their full physical growth.

For most adolescents this is a relatively carefree time. They may work after school and study hard, but there is still time to go to athletic events, participate in school organizations, be active in the community, and spend time with friends. Many parents find this a particularly enjoyable time in their children's lives. They enjoy interesting conversations with them and with their participate in school events, cheer the adolescent's achievements, and appreciate his or her increased freedom and mobility. However, late adolescence can also be a difficult time for teenagers and their parents.

Social Affection versus Self-Esteem

Many late adolescents are still striving to achieve social affection, particularly those who are not members of a peer group of their choice. However, according to Abraham Maslow, more are struggling to meet the need of self-esteem as they maintain the social affection of the peer group. Unfortunately, these two needs are often in conflict.

At times young people seeking social affection may select a path to peer group membership that conflicts with family values. Therefore, acceptance by the group will not lead to self-esteem, but to frustration. For example, if the peer group uses alcohol or drugs and the family does not, the young person will face a conflict of values. When values are in conflict, self-esteem is not possible.

On the other hand, a path that is acceptable to the family may be unpopular with the chosen peer group. For example, a young adult whose family is associated with a particular religious faith may be an outsider in the peer group. Young adult author Norma Fox Mazer writes of this from her own experience: "I was a girl, but not an 'in' girl. I had too many strikes against me: I lived on the wrong side of town. I was Jewish. I had opinions. I didn't know how to make small talk or flirt. I didn't have a steady boyfriend. I was 'serious,' as well, with political ideas. None of these gave me status." So Mazer turned to books and, eventually, to writing to find acceptance.

Too Many Questions

As they get older, adolescents are faced with many issues. They must decide whether or not to attend college and how to pay for it. (In 1991, 62 percent of students graduating from high school enrolled in higher education.) Many must juggle work, studying, and other activities. (Nearly 40 percent of sixteen- through nineteen-year-olds work, at least part time, for pay.) Late adolescents must decide how to spend the money they earn. (In 1990, thirteen- to nineteen-year-olds spent $56 billion on themselves.) Many save their money for college; others share it with their families. Some purchase cars; many buy televisions, stereo equipment, and trendy clothes. For some adolescents having the right car and stylish clothes and going on fancy dates are so important that they work long hours to pay for them, sometimes dropping out of school so they have time to work (of the sixteen- through nineteen-year-olds who work, 60.9 percent are not enrolled in school). Although the school dropout rate is decreasing, nearly one-third of the adolescents who began school four years ago did not graduate with their classmates this year; 20 percent will never graduate from high school.

Most late adolescents are faced with difficult decisions about sexuality and sexual activity. Fifty percent of adolescent women between fifteen and nineteen years of age are sexually experienced. (Nearly 11 percent of fifteen- through nineteen-year-old women became pregnant in the mid 1980s.) The 1988 National Survey of Adolescent Males reported that a third of the boys were sexually active at fifteen, half at sixteen, two-thirds at seventeen, and 86 percent at nineteen. Every year 300,000 babies are born to mothers who have not yet finished high school. Teenage mothers must decide whether or not to keep their babies and whether or not to marry. (Over 55 percent of the unmarried pregnant adolescent girls carried their babies to term.)

Moral Reasoning of the Late Adolescent

Late adolescents need to be prepared to answer the difficult questions they will face and then make decisions based on what is best for their futures. Answering difficult questions such as "Should I take drugs if all of my friends are doing so?" requires mature moral reasoning skills. Psychologist Lawrence Kohlberg contends that the only way to develop one's maturity in moral reasoning is by confronting conflicts one level above the individual's current stage of moral reasoning. Most fifteen-year-olds use what Kohlberg calls conventional moral reasoning, utilizing the laws of adult society so as not to experience guilt and censure. However, if adolescents do not expect to be caught or do not anticipate consequences, their actions may be inappropriate for their long-term benefit. Take, for example, the sixteen-year-old who speeds through a school zone because he thinks no one will catch him. Or the seventeen-year-old who says, "I won't get pregnant if I have intercourse only once." There are far too many tragic examples of the inadequacy of moral reasoning based on following the law simply to avoid guilt and censure.

If adolescents are to answer difficult moral questions successfully, they must move beyond the stage of conventional moral reasoning. The third and final level of moral reasoning, according to Kohlberg, is postconventional moral reasoning. At this more mature stage of moral reasoning, "good and right are matters of individual conscience and involve abstract concepts of justice, human dignity, and equality."

Of course, the adolescent's own value system is based on the values of parents, churches, schools, and communities. The adolescent who has grown up in an environment where there are rules, responsibilities, and accountability for actions taken is much more likely to develop postconventional moral reasoning than the adolescent who has experienced neither expectations nor consequences.

Because development of postconventional moral reasoning occurs only if the adolescent has passed through the stage of conventional moral reasoning and if she or he has confronted complex issues requiring higher moral reasoning, it is important that parents not attempt to shield older adolescents from making complex ethical decisions. Most parents would prefer that their adolescent children avoid difficult situations in which ethical decision making is required. However, it is impossible and inappropriate to protect adolescents entirely from these situations. If adolescents do not confront ethical dilemmas while at home and at school, they will have severe difficulty doing so as independent adults. Of course, parents do not want to engineer difficult dilemmas for adolescents. Parents can, however, prepare adolescents for dealing with ethical decisions by discussing difficult issues with them; allowing them the freedom to make more and more decisions about friends, jobs, and social events; and encouraging them to read and discuss books that pose difficult ethical dilemmas.

. . . . . .

The Late Adolescent Reader

Late adolescents who read for pleasure are well on the road to becoming mature, adult readers. They are willing to exert considerable effort in reading and to tackle increasingly challenging books. At times they will take on particularly difficult books simply to meet the challenge.

The Joy of Reading

When maturing readers are willing to try reading almost anything, Margaret Early says they have entered the aesthetic stage of reading (see chart in chapter 1, p. 9). Aesthetic readers read for the joy of reading and to meet a variety of purposes: for pleasure, to gain general knowledge, to locate specific information, to learn more about a topic, to learn a new skill. They are likely to be reading several books at one time. According to Early's studies, the aesthetic stage is rarely reached before the late high school years; often it is never reached. Recent statistics seem to confirm this, as they show that the average adult in the United States reads only 1.2 books per year and spends six hours per week in a shopping mall and only one hour per week reading.

According to Early, if readers are to reach the aesthetic stage, they must pass through the egocentric stage with minimal difficulty. If they skip a stage, they are unlikely to progress to the next stage of reading development.

Egocentric Needs Still Present

Most late adolescents still select books that meet their egocentric needs, with young characters and realistic plots. We can continue to suggest these books to them. Look for books with characters who are a year or two older than the reader and who are beginning to face increasingly adult problems. As teenagers' interests begin to broaden, we can suggest a wider range of books on more adult topics.

It is important to note that maturing readers can be at more than one stage of reading development at a time. It is possible, for example, for young adults to continue to read books with young characters and simple, straightforward plots while beginning to tackle more difficult works of literature. This flexibility is the sign of an aesthetic reader.

The period of late adolescence is the final bridge from childhood to adulthood. For most adolescents it is a time of great enthusiasm, significant learning, and wonderful fun. For others, however, it is a period in which the difficult decisions they are unprepared to make push them into premature adulthood. Par-

ents can help by providing adolescents with guidance while helping them confront difficult issues with justice and accountability.
Books written by skilled authors can help adolescents pose and
answer some of the most compelling questions of young adulthood. Late adolescents who read for pleasure are not only on the
way to becoming adult readers, but are more likely to confront
the moral dilemmas in their own lives with mature moral reasoning.

4

. . . .

Encouraging Teens and Preteens to Read

*The things young people want to read are related to their
chronological age regardless of the level of their reading ability.
Even if they have one foot in the world of adult literature, one foot
will remain in the literature of childhood. I remember that one of
my daughters, the summer before she reached sixteen, not only
read* War and Peace—*at that time I had not read it—but also
Maureen Daly's* Seventeenth Summer. Jeannette H. Eyerly

Why Good Readers Quit Reading

The peak of reading interest often occurs around age twelve; that
is also the age when many readers lose interest in books. This
happens for several reasons. Young readers are required by
schools or pushed by parents to read books for which they are
not emotionally and intellectually ready. Many adolescents have
difficulty finding books with young characters who face the problems of adolescence. Conversely, adolescents are gaining emotional and intellectual maturity, but the books they are reading
are not keeping up with their maturity, and they do not know
how to locate more appropriate books. Many parents, teachers,
and librarians are unaware of appropriate books to recommend.

Some adults discourage adolescents from selecting books on certain topics or themes of interest. (One mother limits her teenage daughter's reading to books with "happy endings." Not surprisingly, the girl rarely reads.) For some adolescents, reading is not accepted by their peer group. And, for some whose reading ability has not kept up with their emotional and physical maturity, struggling through books provides an additional frustration.

What Parents Can Do to Keep Adolescents Reading

If we are aware of these stumbling blocks and understand our adolescent's egocentric reading interests, we can encourage the beginning of mature, aesthetic reading patterns. There are several things parents can do: Make reading fun, never push, and encourage a wide range of reading interests.

In a wonderful book, *In the Middle: Writing, Reading, and Learning with Adolescents*, about how she has turned twelve- and thirteen-year-old students into readers and writers, Nancie Atwell claims that all adolescents can be good readers. She maintains that there is no great secret to helping adolescents become good readers: They must read a lot and discuss what they have read with other readers. Atwell reports that her middle school students in Maine read more than thirty-five books per year. They do this because their classroom is an environment filled with books they want to read. Over and over the students report to her that their freedom to choose what they read has turned them into readers. And, Atwell points out, they are free to choose from "novels and short stories written expressly for young adults, adolescent literature of . . . breadth and depth" (p. 161).

Finally, says Atwell, young readers, like all readers, need to have the opportunity to talk about the books they read. Reading, particularly for adolescents, must have a social dimension. Even if the adolescent is not in a classroom filled with books, parents can help them become readers by following some simple guidelines.

Make books available. Go to libraries and bookstores to find books for your teens. Use the bibliographic listings in chapters 11 and 12 to help you locate appropriate books. Fill your home with books.

Allow your teenager to select books. Don't fall into the trap of assuming that because you remember liking a particular book at a particular age, the adolescent will like it too. For one thing, our memory tends to be faulty about when we actually read certain books. Secondly, we often remember liking a book when we read it, but actually we only learned to like the book much later. These two facts have become increasingly clear to me in a course on adolescent literature that I teach to adults. The students are asked to write down the title of a book they loved as a young adult; the titles they list tend to be classics. Later in the class I give them the following assignment: Reread the book you loved as a youth and select a current book on a similar theme to read and compare to it. This assignment never fails to produce groans as many of the adults ask, "Do I have to read the whole book I read as a teenager?" Often they even admit, "I guess I must have been older when I read that book; may I select a different one?"

Ask your teenager to recommend a favorite book to you. Read a book recommended by your adolescent child and discuss it with her or him. Be careful not to be judgmental about the choice.

Help make reading fun. For example, we must remember that preadolescents need to play with language, and we should encourage books in which language is fun. Joke books are often a good bridge to higher levels of reading development. Comic books serve the same function for some youngsters. Parents shouldn't discourage preadolescents from reading these books. Instead, we can help our preteenagers broaden this interest by suggesting humorous young adult books like Paula Danziger's *The Cat Ate My Gymsuit*, which is particularly appropriate for young teenage girls, or Roald Dahl's *Charlie and the Chocolate Factory*. Many of the books listed in chapter 11 relate to the preadolescent's interests and needs and include playful use of language.

Never push. Don't push young readers beyond what they are willing to tackle. Many girls are interested in romance and parents should not discourage this interest. In fact, we can encourage it by suggesting some young adult romances of high literary quality. (Most of the "love and romance" books discussed in chapter 11 fall into this category.) This keeps girls reading and at the same time helps them mature in their literary tastes. To help broaden adolescents' reading interests, we should look carefully at the books they select. For example, readers who read romances may have enjoyed several Gothic romance novels. These books are set in another time, in a distant land, and contain many of the literary conceits of mystery novels. We might help these readers broaden their reading interests by introducing them to young adult historical fiction and mystery. (Books in all of these genres are suggested in chapter 11.)

Encourage a wide range of reading interests. Parents should encourage a wide range of reading interests in teenagers. Many of us praise our children when they select adult, classic works, but we say little or even criticize them when they select young adult books. It is important to remember that the aesthetic reader, who is becoming a mature adult reader, has a broad range of reading interests. The young adult who reads a Judy Blume novel over the weekend, picks up *Gone with the Wind* in the library on Monday, and reads *Seventeen* magazine that evening is becoming an aesthetic reader. We should encourage all of these reading interests.

Encourage adolescents to exchange and discuss books with friends. Ask your teenager to share a book he or she has enjoyed with a good friend. If summer reading groups are available at local public libraries or through bookstores, suggest that the teenager might want to try them out. Don't push, don't require, simply make the activity an option. Encourage discussions about books while you are driving adolescents to and from activities or while friends are visiting. Don't hesitate to ask your teenager and his or her friends, "Read any good books lately?"

Encouraging Reluctant Readers

Unfortunately, some adolescents rarely read, not because they can't but because they won't. Some quit reading altogether. As standardized test results show, adolescents who do not read for pleasure are not likely to continue to progress as readers. These reluctant readers are unlikely to develop mature, aesthetic reading patterns; they are likely to become nonreading adults. After studying and analyzing a group of seventh-grade reluctant readers, G. Kylene Beers divided them into three groups:

Dormant readers—Adolescents who like to read, identify themselves as readers, express positive feelings about others who enjoy reading, but do not presently make much time to read.

Uncommitted readers—Teenagers who do not like to read, do not identify themselves as readers, express positive feeling about others who enjoy reading, and suggest they may read in the future.

Unmotivated readers—Readers who do not like to read, do not identify themselves as readers, express negative feelings about those who enjoy reading, and do not plan to read in the future.

Why Some Young People Dislike Reading

A study by Lance Gentile and Merna McMillan can help us understand why some young people who are capable of reading better are reluctant to read. That understanding and Beers's identification of the different types of reluctant readers can provide parents with some clues as to how to deal with teenagers who dislike reading. According to Gentile and McMillan:

Many adolescents equate reading with ridicule, failure, or exclusively school-related tasks. If this is true of your adolescent, you can help by providing an example that reading is fun. Parents who read for pleasure are more likely to have children who read for pleasure. Encourage nonreading adolescents to purchase magazines in areas that interest them. Be sure your youngster sees you reading magazines. Buy paperback books and read them. When you purchase a book, ask if your teenager would like to buy one too. It is important to remember that the only way to get out of the nonreading habit is to read. Don't push adolescents into books they are unwilling to tackle; encourage them to read magazines or books they will enjoy and make such reading material available.

Some people are not excited by ideas. Many adolescents are driven to experience life directly, rather than through reading. In fact, as adolescents mature the time they have for pleasure reading diminishes. Maturing adolescents become more and more involved in activities, school, work, and socializing with friends. Social interaction is one of a teenager's most basic needs, and it is difficult to interact with others while reading a book. Adults need to help adolescents see that books can make life more exciting. For example, if your son and his friends plan to go white-water rafting, you can purchase a book on the topic or check one out of the library for him. He may begin to see that reading about the experience can enhance his enjoyment of it.

A great number of adolescents do not want to sit, and in some cases are incapable of sitting, for prolonged periods. Adolescence is one of the most physically active periods of life. Parents, particularly of youngsters just entering puberty, should keep this in mind when selecting or suggesting reading material. Magazines are good for young adolescents since the articles are short and are aimed at the egocentric reading needs of teenagers. Most young adult books have short chapters that begin with "hooks" to encourage the reader to keep reading and end with "clinchers" to make the reader turn to the next chapter.

Adolescence is a time of intense egocentrism. Young adult literature encourages teenagers to keep reading. Unfortunately, most reading and English programs in middle, junior, and senior high schools do not encourage the reading of young adult books. In fact, many of these programs require the reading of classics that are often far removed from the egocentric needs of young readers. These programs, designed to develop mature readers, often keep adolescents from becoming mature readers by ignoring their egocentric stage of reading development. Parents can help by introducing adolescents to young adult books. (Chapters 11 and 12 are designed to help you do so.)

Many young people demand to be entertained. Young adult books should solve the problem of the "boring" book. Young adults demand entertainment, and young adult books provide it. Adolescents often like to read books directly related to movies or television shows they watch. If an adolescent has seen a particular movie or enjoys a television show, you can check bookstores to see if appropriate books are available. An increasing number of movies that appeal to adolescents are based on young adult novels. Bookstores market the books by making this connection obvious.

Many adolescents are pressured to read. It is difficult for parents and teachers to encourage young people to read without pressuring them. The line between the two is thin, but encouragement has some characteristics that help to distinguish it from pressure. In an encouraging atmosphere, parents and teachers are aware of adolescents' interests and needs and seek books addressing these. A wide variety of reading material is available, including young adult books. Adolescents are allowed to select their own reading materials. Adults pay more attention to the fact that youngsters are reading than to what they are reading.

Many young people grow up in a atmosphere where there is no reading material, but it is never too late to change the environment. Inexpensive books can be purchased at used bookstores; library cards are usually free. Children model their parents' actions; if we read, our children are likely to read.

Reading is considered antisocial by many adolescents, particularly if the teenager is part of a nonreading peer group. This may be the hardest trend to reverse. Parents can help by attempting to discover acceptable reading material. Sometimes magazines, "how-to" books, or comic books are of interest to the peer group when books are not. Many teenagers are more willing to accept paperback books than hardcover books, which may look too much like textbooks. Paperback publishers work hard to develop covers that appeal to adolescents. Adolescents who rarely read are most likely to be attracted to covers that are realistic and similar to magazine covers. Another way to get teenagers to read is to select material that relates to peer group interest. If the peer group is interested in cars, try to find books about cars and auto mechanics. A youngster who learns about cars through books may become more acceptable to the peer group. An increasing number of adolescents choose computer games over books for occupying their free time. Parents can seek out computer magazines and books that extend the young person's knowledge of computers beyond the games and even improve his or her ability to play the games.

Some adolescents view reading as part of the adult world and reject it. For some adolescents, anything that appears to be adult is unacceptable. This problem usually decreases as the young person grows older. If your teenager has always been a reader, if your house is filled with books, and if you read, it is likely your youngster will grow into a reader. Parents must avoid pushing; the more we push teenagers toward books, the more they will run from them.

Some adolescents do not know how to locate things they want to read. Beers suggests that although choice of books continues to be important to reluctant readers, choosing from a narrower field of books can be helpful. Sometimes having a whole library of books from which to select can be intimidating to teenagers who rarely read. Therefore, parents might suggest a section of a bookstore or library from which the adolescent can select a book. Or, two or three books on topics of potential interest to the adolescent might be brought home so that the range of choices is smaller. Beers also suggests that reluctant readers are more interested in books with illustrations and are usually willing to listen to an entire book read aloud. Reluctant readers are also more likely to be interested in books related to movies or television shows or activities in which they are interested, as well as in magazines and joke books.

. . . . . .

Helping Teens Who Can't Read

If your teenager is a poor reader, it is even more urgent that you get him or her to read. This will be more difficult because your child has been defeated by books, but it is more important because the only way to improve reading skills is to read.

Techniques that Work (Sometimes)

As a teacher of adolescents, I've tried all kinds of techniques with teenagers who don't read because they can't read. I've shown them studies that prove that the better people read, the more money they earn over a lifetime. I've tried to teach reading through learning to read the driver's manual and income tax forms. I've asked students to level with me: "Why can't you read? You're smart. What happened?" And, I have introduced them to books that are written on lower reading levels but have mature themes. I have had success with all of these techniques, but the success has been limited to a few individuals.

I sympathize with parents of adolescents who face this problem. Nothing is more frustrating than trying to convince someone to do something when that person is convinced that he or she knows better than you, particularly when that person is your adolescent child. I also understand the major reason why these poor readers resist learning to read; I am not so different myself. I know I cannot roller-skate, so don't suggest roller-blading; I won't even attempt it. Like many adolescents, I'd rather fail by not trying, so I can justify my defeat by saying, "I didn't want to do it anyway. Roller-blading is dumb, and it's dangerous to my health." Poor readers are very good at justifying their failure when they don't try, but unfortunately that does not solve their problem. In the end, they still can't read.

Admitting the problem is the first step. Honesty is the first step toward helping youngsters tackle their reading problems. They have to admit they cannot read, or at least not well. I usually begin by asking them to tell me about their reading experiences. "What is it about reading that makes it so difficult?" I avoid preaching or judging. I try to understand their problems. It helps to remember that there are many things I cannot and will not do.

Discussing the problem. By discussing the problem, we've admitted that it exists. Many young people, once they've admitted that not being able to read is a problem, are willing to try to improve their reading skills. I let them know it will not be easy. I encourage them and express my appreciation for even the smallest achievement. Learning to read is very difficult; it is more difficult for young adults than it is for children. Many young adults no longer experience the unconscious enjoyment children find in playing with language. For them, there is little except humiliation in the process.

Getting help. If you have an adolescent with a severe reading problem, get help. Going through the process described above with your own child is almost impossible; a tutor can help. Many schools and communities provide free or inexpensive tutoring for adolescents and adults. Often, the principal or guidance counselor in your child's school can help you find a tutoring service.

Finding materials for poor readers. A major difficulty for parents with teenagers who do not read well is finding material they can read that is not too juvenile. "How-to" books about topics of interest and/or magazines that deal with sports or other interests sometimes appeal to poor readers. Also within the field of young adult literature there is a classification known as high interest/easy reading. These books are designed to be easy to read but to appeal to the maturity level of the young adult. Many school and public libraries have bibliographic guides to these books. I'll suggest some in chapter 7. Books in this classification appear with an asterisk in chapters 11 and 12.

By preadolescence, most readers are capable of reading independently. The peak of their interest in reading often occurs around age twelve. However, this is also the age when some adolescents turn away from reading. Adolescents will only continue to read if it helps meet their needs for social acceptance and self-esteem. Books and reading can help meet these needs if parents continue to encourage reading by accepting the adolescent's developing reading interests, encouraging the adolescent to choose from a wide variety of books, and discussing the books with the adolescent and her or his friends.

Parents with adolescents who don't read or can't read have a more difficult task. They need to understand why their adolescent children don't or can't read. Parents may be able to encourage their teenagers to continue reading by making available the right reading material at the right time and providing appropriate help when needed.

TWO

. . . .

Sharing Books

5

. . . .

Reading Aloud and Discussing Books

The art of living cannot be taught or learned by rote, so I believe that we should encourage our children to make inquiry and seek answers, directly, with honesty, through reading and open discussion in the home as well as at school. Alice Childress

Reading Aloud

Reading aloud is an excellent way to involve the entire family in books. Although many people believe that reading aloud is something done only with small children, the advantages are so great that parents of adolescents should consider building a reading aloud tradition in their families. Before you say "that's impossible," let's discuss why it is so important.

Why Read Aloud?

Earlier in this century, many families gathered in the evenings to listen to one another read. Often the Bible was the primary work shared, but as more books became available families shared the classic works of literature. After the advent of radio and television, the practice of reading aloud became increasingly rare. In recent years educators have begun to understand the tragedy of this loss.

Jim Trelease's *The New Read-Aloud Handbook* and similar books have encouraged parents of young children to reexamine their oral reading practices. It is time for parents of adolescents to consider the important benefits of this simple, enjoyable pastime.

One reason to read aloud is that it is fun. Skilled readers can captivate audiences of all ages by reading aloud from carefully selected books. Each listener pictures characters and settings differently, thereby fulfilling individual needs. As Trelease says in *Read All About It! Great Read-Aloud Stories, Poems & Newspaper Pieces for Preteens and Teens*, one of the major factors in becoming a lifetime reader is to think of reading as fun. "Human beings—be they five-year-olds or fifty-five-year-olds—will only do over and over what brings them pleasure."

There are many educational benefits to reading aloud. It can improve skill in reading and listening, foster positive attitudes toward reading, encourage imagination, develop reading maturity, and help bring a family together.

To improve reading skills. Poor readers often read word for word and are unable to understand what they read. They may have difficulty pronouncing words. Their reading skills usually do not keep up with their intellectual and emotional growth. Listening to books read aloud can help poor readers improve their silent reading skills. They hear material that is appropriate to their intellectual and emotional maturity. They hear books as they were meant to be read, and this serves as a model for them. As they listen, they must recall the details of the story and interpret the author's intent. In all of these ways, listening to a work read orally helps young people strengthen their own reading skills.

To improve listening skills. Hearing books read aloud improves listening skills. Teachers often complain that students are not good listeners and that their attention spans are short. One way to increase attention span is by listening to a book of action, suspense, or humor.

To foster a positive attitude toward reading. Parents who enjoy the experience of reading aloud to their family create positive reading models. Readers who have negative attitudes toward reading are likely to have difficulty reading and understanding what they read.

At some time, all of us have experienced personal attitude problems. Perhaps you have taken a course you did not want to take. Every time you picked up the textbook to study, you found your mind wandering. Overcoming a negative attitude is the first step to reading and understanding. The same is true for adolescents.

For some adolescents, a book they hear read aloud is the first book they have "read" all the way through. The sense of accomplishment that comes from reading an entire book, even if it is read to the adolescent, can be enough to create a positive attitude toward reading. For others, an oral reading selection might be the first book of suspense, fantasy, humor, or science fiction they have enjoyed. The experience may open new reading doors. Listening to a new author for the first time may make a listener search for more books by the same author.

We know that immature readers are more likely to select familiar books than totally new books. Many young readers read the same book repeatedly. The reading aloud experience can open up adolescents to new books, new authors, and new genres to explore. Reading aloud expands reading horizons.

To foster imagination. Studies have found that typical children watch between six and eight hours of TV per day. Teenagers who watch a great deal of television or play endless computer games may lose their ability to create images. Television and computer games create images for the viewer or the player, while reading requires readers to create their own images.

Listening to stories and books read orally helps young people develop their ability to imagine. Characters and place take shape in listeners' imaginations. The importance of imagination cannot be underestimated. A person who cannot create images cannot read because reading requires taking symbols and letters from a page and turning them into words and sentences to create an image. The person who cannot imagine has difficulty dealing with life's problems because solving problems requires imagining solutions. Hearing books read aloud helps adolescents move from the artificial images of TV and video games to more demanding reading material that requires a well-developed ability to imagine.

To develop reading maturity. Reading aloud allows adults to share stories with youngsters who do not yet read well enough to read them on their own. Adolescents can participate when great works of literature are read orally. All educators who advocate reading aloud agree that it is important to share wonderful books with youngsters before they are able to read them themselves. The reader's inflection and emphasis allow the adolescent to put meaning to words and stories too complex for silent reading. Young adult author Madeleine L'Engle reflects on reading Shakespeare aloud to her preadolescent children and grandchildren when she writes about their adult love of great literature and their fluency with language.

My observation of young readers convinces me that reading maturity develops in most avid silent readers, as well as in those who have been read to. However, it does not develop as rapidly in youngsters who have not been read to on a regular basis. There are two reasons for this. First, adults who read aloud usually select exceptionally well-written books with good plots and good characterization, which adolescents would not necessarily discover on their own. As they listen, youngsters begin to gain a taste for this type of literature. Second, the language of books often is more impressive when read and heard aloud than when read silently. Good readers often skim books they read silently, losing the subtlety of the author's language and style. Poor readers, on the other hand, may be unable to hear the language as they struggle to understand what the author is saying. Enjoying language is central to the experience of listening.

To encourage family togetherness. Recently I overheard a group of middle and high school teachers discussing their students' home lives. A major concern was how little time adolescents spend with their families. Numerous teachers said it was not unusual for their students to go home to an empty house, eat a sandwich, then go to work. The household with one or two working parents is the norm rather than the exception. Many adolescents are involved in after-school activities or have jobs. Often, busy schedules prevent families from eating meals together.

All of us recognize the potential problems that arise when communication between parents and youngsters is limited to only a few minutes a day. Recent surveys show that parents and adolescents rarely talk about substantive topics—most of their talk involves parents relating instructions and directions to the adolescent.

Many adolescents find speaking to their parents difficult, and parents experience similar frustration. In part, this communication gap is due to normal changes in the adolescent's attitudes and her or his push for increased independence from the family. Problems in communication also occur because parents and adolescents rarely attempt to communicate. This may be because of limited time spent together or it may be a result of lack of practice. The more difficult the communication, the more likely parents and teens will attempt to avoid it. However, there is no more important time than adolescence to keep the lines of communication between parents and children open.

Not all families grow apart during the years children are adolescents; many strengthen their relationships. The key to improved relationships appears to be the time that each family member, including adolescents, commits to the family: evening meals, common activities, vacations. Even when time is reserved, communication is not always open. Reading aloud together can open up new lines of communication between parents and adolescents.

. . . . . .

A Family Read-Aloud Program

If your family does not normally read together, here is a simple plan for beginning a read-aloud program.

A good place to get into the oral reading habit is on a long car trip. If you can locate a good book about the place you are going to visit, reading it aloud in the car is natural. The ensuing conversation makes the miles speed by. If a book about your destination is not available, you might read about just one part of your trip, such as a zoo or aquarium.

Of course, the book need not deal with the vacation. It could be one of general family interest. On one of my family's most relaxing, enjoyable vacations we read Richard Adams's *Watership Down*, a book written to be read aloud. In fact, it is based on stories the author told his children as they traveled through Great Britain.

Holidays and birthdays are natural times to begin a reading-aloud tradition. We have friends who each select a special poem to read at the birthday dinner of the celebrant. The tradition began when the parents were first married and continued with the birth of each of their children.

Holidays are made for traditions, particularly Christmas and Hanukkah. There are thousands of stories and poems available for these occasions. It's fun for different family members to select at least one new story or poem each year. Several years ago I discovered Barbara Robinson's hilariously funny *The Best Christmas Pageant Ever*. We enjoyed it so much that we've read it every

Christmas ever since, this year sharing it with three generations of my husband's family as we gathered around our Christmas tree.

Building a Family Read-Aloud Tradition

Once a family read-aloud tradition is begun, it is easy to continue. Since the initial experience was enjoyable, it is natural to suggest that it continue on a regular basis.

The key to making a family oral reading time successful is to do it regularly. Reading aloud is habit forming; once the habit is formed, it is hard to break. But first, the family must agree on an appropriate time for reading, a time convenient for all family members. Once the time is set, each family member must reserve that time. If one consistently misses the reading time, others will do the same.

After the time has been set, the first book should be chosen jointly, or the family should agree that the first reader be given the privilege of selecting a book. Choosing a book that is appropriate for the entire family is very important. Try to observe these guidelines.

- Select the book jointly or allow the reader to select a book.
- Be sure the book is appropriate for the reader's skill and the listeners' interest.
- Select a book with a fast-paced plot. Look at the first few paragraphs. Are you immediately caught up in the story?
- Select a book with well-rounded characters who develop with the story. Be sure that listeners can identify with the characters.
- Dialogue should be easy to read. Avoid dialect that is not natural to the reader.
- Select a book with few descriptive passages, at least initially.
- If either reader or listeners are not enjoying the book after the first reading, find a different book.

- Do not hesitate to select a book that the listeners could not read themselves.
- If you can't find a book, try a magazine or newspaper article that will appeal to the listeners.

Reading the Book

If possible, the reader should preread the book; often the most successful read-aloud book is one the reader loves. It is much easier to read aloud a book you enjoy than one you do not. If, however, you select a book with which you are unfamiliar and decide after the first oral reading session that you are not comfortable with it, choose another book. In my family, books are not always preread. After the first oral reading we make a joint decision about whether to continue. Often we orally read magazine or newspaper articles we think are likely to be of interest. Reading aloud should be a pleasure, not a struggle. If readers or listeners are not enjoying the book or the article, stop reading it.

All members of the family who are able to read should have an opportunity to read or to select a book to be read. One reader should read the entire book. If younger readers are uncomfortable reading an entire book they might select a short story or poem.

All family members should be involved in oral reading. It is often difficult for young children to sit still, so the reading time should be adjusted to their needs. They can be given paper and crayons to illustrate the story as they listen. Even young children should be encouraged to select books they want read. If children are too young to be a regular part of reading sessions, they can be the focus of it when appropriate material is read. Younger members of the family provide a wonderful audience for adolescent readers, who can select books specifically for their younger siblings. Many children's books are enjoyable to the whole family. Jim Trelease's *The New Read-Aloud Handbook* is a fantastic resource for finding children's books with wide appeal.

Finding a Location for Reading Aloud

Read-aloud sessions should be held in a comfortable place. The reader needs to have a comfortable chair and good light. Listeners should be comfortable and in a position to see and hear the reader. The location should be selected to ensure a minimum of interruptions. Reading outside may seem ideal, but a barking dog or a buzzing bee can be an annoying distraction. We can't read with our family dogs present, because they are far too demanding of our attention. If you select a time when there are numerous phone calls, you might want to take the phone off the hook. Constant interruptions limit the pleasure of the experience.

· · · · · ·

Discussing Books and Articles

Books or articles read aloud can inspire parent-adolescent discussions. Talking about incidents, characters, problems, and relationships in books or issues presented in the articles can be a natural way to begin a discussion about important topics that may be difficult to discuss. Recently, during a long car trip, my husband and I had a fascinating conversation with our two adolescent nieces about Bette Greene's *The Drowning of Stephan Jones*, whose plot revolves around the issues of peer pressure, stereotyping, prejudice, and gay bashing. Parents and children who have been talking about books for years find the transition from discussing children's books to discussing young adult books quite easy. However, parents who are just beginning to discuss books with adolescents may find that they resist attempts at discussion. It is important that the discussion occur as naturally as possible.

Discussion is impossible unless there is something to discuss. Books read together, either orally or silently, can fill that need. Consider the following points as you plan for book discussions.

- Books or articles should relate to common interests of parents and adolescents.
- Avoid books on topics within the parent's area of expertise. Adolescents cannot discuss such topics on an equal basis.
- Nonfiction books or articles in areas of the adolescent's expertise are a good choice.
- Try to choose a type of book that interests the adolescent (mystery, science fiction, adventure).
- Discussing the adolescent's favorite book is a good way to begin.
- Books by an author the adolescent has previously enjoyed are a good choice.
- Initially, avoid books or articles on controversial topics or issues about which you and your teenager do not agree. However, as you become more comfortable discussing books, difficult issues should become a regular part of your repertoire.
- Books should be worth discussing.

How to Discuss a Book

Discussion should flow naturally from common interests and concerns. This is easiest when the book is within an area of new interest for both parent and adolescent. If this is the case, both the adolescent and the parent can meet and discuss the book as relative equals.

Louise Rosenblatt, a researcher and educator who has examined how readers respond to literature, suggests that there is a hierarchy of response. As readers become more comfortable discussing books, they move from less mature levels of response to more complex responses. The lower levels of the response hierarchy include such things as simple emotional responses ("I didn't like the book") and simple descriptions of what happened in the book ("First . . . , and then . . ."). Higher levels of response to a book or article include such things as inferring meaning ("I think the author really means . . ."), explaining the motivation of characters ("He was doing that because . . ."), making connections to the reader's own life ("I remember a time when Grandpa was sick like the grandfather in the book"), interpreting overall theme or meaning ("The author really wrote the book to show how cruel people can be to each other"), and judging literary quality ("I didn't think the characters in the book were as realistic as the characters in his other books"). Rosenblatt suggests that we should expect lower levels of response either when the particular book or article is too mature for the reader or when the reader is inexperienced in discussing books. Here are some ways that you can encourage your adolescent to learn to respond more maturely to books she or he is reading.

Allow the adolescent to be the expert. If the book is in an area about which you know a lot, be careful not to preach. Initiate the discussion by allowing the adolescent to take control. For example, suppose your daughter is interested in cooking. You are a gourmet cook, so you suggest a particular cookbook to her. She reads it but doesn't say anything about it. You initiate a discussion by asking, "What did you think of his approach to baking bread?" She answers, "You never make bread without yeast, Mom." She is recognizing your expertise. "I know," you answer. "I've been afraid to try something new, but I'd like to. Would you help me?" You have found an area in which she can be the expert (or at least more nearly equal).

Don't force the discussion. Discussions should not be forced, but the questions you pose must lead to more than simple "yes" or "no" answers. You and your son have read Lois Duncan's *Killing Mr. Griffin*. You ask him, "What did you think of the book?" He says, "It was OK." Not a lot of room for discussion here. Try a new tack. "At first I thought Mark was a bit unrealistic, but then I remembered a kid in my high school class who could convince anyone to do anything." This simple comment might produce, "Yeah, there's a kid in my class like that." Or, it might produce silence. Try again. "What do you think? Are there really people like Mark?" If he answers with grunts, don't attempt to force the discussion. Wait. He may mention the book later, or maybe he didn't find anything in it worth discussing.

Encourage the adolescent to take the lead as often as possible. If you know your son has some knowledge that might lead to a good discussion of *Killing Mr. Griffin*, begin by encouraging him to use his knowledge. "Aren't you taking psychology this year? Did you study psychotic behavior? Is Duncan's characterization of a psychotic accurate?"

Remain open to the adolescent's opinions. Avoid being judgmental, but encourage clarification. Your son answers, "It was a dumb book." You respond, "Why do you think so? Do you think Duncan's portrayal of Mark was inaccurate?" Many teenagers have learned how to cut off conversations with adults by making what appear to be dead-end comments. Avoid getting angry and saying things like, "How could you say that?" Try to open all avenues by asking questions that require justification.

Be honest. Let the adolescent take the lead, expressing opinions and justifying them. If you disagree, simply state your disagreement and explain why, but respect your adolescent's opinion. You say, "I disagree with you on that point. I think there are personalities like Mark. There's a guy in my office who is a lot like Mark. What do you think? Am I way off base here?"

Don't push uncomfortable subjects. Avoid controversial or embarrassing subjects addressed in the book. If the discussion is going well, bring them up when you are both comfortable in the conversation. Don't push the adolescent, but do not avoid topics that need to be discussed. Be patient. If you have successfully opened the lines of communication, it will be much easier to bring up these topics later. You and your son have been discussing the character of Mark on and off for several days. On several occasions he has initiated the discussion. "See that kid over there? He's the one I told you is sort of like a Mark personality." Or, you are concerned about the things you hear some of the kids saying about their teachers. You say, "One thing that really bothered me is that it seemed acceptable for those kids to be so mean to Mr. Griffin. Not one of the kids ever came to his defense. Surely some of them saw some virtue in what he was doing. I've come to respect some of the teachers I thought were mean when I was a kid." Leave plenty of room for him to enter the conversation. Perhaps he will express some similar concerns. If he doesn't, don't push. Sometimes just mentioning the topic is enough.

Treat the adolescent as an equal in the discussion. Throughout discussions with adolescents you must assume the same role as do authors of young adult books. Allow the teen to come to his or her own decision. Ask good questions, but avoid giving answers. Be careful not to talk down. Be honest in expressing your opinions, and justify them in the same way you expect the young adult to justify his or her opinions. Be sensitive to the needs of the adolescent.

Discuss books you haven't read. Encourage your teenager to discuss books with you even if you haven't read them. Ask "What are you reading? What's it about?" If your adolescent brings up an interesting topic, you might interject information about a book you have read on a similar topic.

Discuss books the adolescent has not read. Don't hesitate to talk to your adolescent about books you are reading that she or he has not read. I told my fourteen-year-old niece Stephanie about Bruce Courtenay's compelling adult novel *The Power of One*. Although the book is likely to have some appeal to early adolescents because the protagonist grows from a very young boy to a young adult, it is a hard-hitting account of the beginning of apartheid in South Africa and is far longer and more complex than young adult books. However, after our discussion she asked if she could read it. I said, "Sure, if you tell me what you think about it after you've read it." She read it, loved it, and although she missed some of the political nuances, she was captured by the powerful story and has expressed a new interest in South Africa.

How to Begin a Discussion about a Book
Initiate the discussion; don't wait for the adolescent to do so.

- Select a common area of interest in which you are *not* an expert.
- Avoid questions that lead to "yes" or "no" answers.
- Avoid judgmental comments about the book or the teen's opinions. Make comments that will open doors for further discussion.
- Ask questions that encourage the expressing of an opinion. Avoid giving answers.
- Encourage the adolescent to take the lead in the discussion; select an area of his/her expertise to discuss.
- Remain open to the adolescent's opinions, but ask for clarification and justification.
- Express your own opinions honestly. Be careful not to cut off differing opinions.
- Initially, avoid controversial or embarrassing subjects.
- Be patient, don't push, avoid getting angry.

Reading aloud as a family and discussing topics based on reading can improve communication between parents and adolescents. Often communication gaps are caused by lack of time spent communicating rather than by inherent differences. Parents who keep the lines of communication open by sharing common interests and expressing respect for adolescents' opinions are likely to understand better the problems of the young and to narrow the generation gap.

6

The Electronic Age of Reading

Isn't it interesting that with all the marvelous computerized and transistorized accomplishments of TV we've yet to hear any of the hostages say, "Thank God we had TV! It got us through our darkest hours. We could never have survived without it."

Jim Trelease, commenting on the release of
the American hostages held by Iran

The Influence of Television

Television is a paradox. By the time they finish high school, most students have spent more time watching TV than they have spent doing anything else except sleeping. Television (including cable TV and videocassettes) is our most popular form of entertainment. It is the great equalizer; our access to it has little to do with our economic, social, or educational status. It shapes our lives.

And yet, we condemn television. We call it boring, stupid, simplistic. We blame it for children's reading problems and lack of attention in school, broken families, overemphasis on sports, and even violence. Why?

Television can be destructive, but only if we allow it to be. Almost all studies of television have concluded that it can be a positive force when viewers actively select what they view. Parents must teach children to control TV, rather than allowing TV to control them. But how?

Making Television a Literacy Experience

If we limit access to television and select programs carefully, TV viewing can encourage adolescents to read. Educator Harlan Hamilton conducted a study in which junior high school students were given a choice between reading books related to TV programs or reading other books. More than two-thirds of the students selected the television-related books. Likewise, 89 percent of students in a Virginia study said their choice to read a book had been influenced by its related television program. Other studies have found that television and movies are more likely to motivate youngsters to read books than are teachers, parents, or peers. This can be seen even in more mature readers. In 1990 a survey of college students indicated that many of the books they chose to read for pleasure were related to current popular movies. If you check the best-seller list on any given Sunday, you will find that among the best-selling books, particularly paperback fiction, are those that have been turned into current popular movies. Television and movies affect what adolescents and adults alike read for pleasure.

Parents, teachers, and librarians can use the interest in and enjoyment of television and movies to get young people to read. To do this we must overcome our bias against TV and learn to make it work for us. Among other things, this means we must become selective viewers, limiting the amount of television we watch.

Book Tie-ins

The television and publishing industries capitalize on television's ability to influence reading by producing media tie-ins, a term used to describe books related to media. The tie-ins take several forms: books on which TV shows or movies are based; books based on scripts; books about media celebrities, special events, development of a TV series, and the subjects treated in TV shows; and the actual scripts of television shows and movies.

The three major networks, cable networks, and many pay-for-view channels are involved in book/television tie-in programs. Because the programming changes frequently and is not offered in all markets, the best way for parents and adolescents to keep up with quality programming is to read *TV Guide* or a similar program listing.

In addition to special programming for children and young adults, all the networks and many cable and pay-for-view networks present prime-time programming based on books appropriate for adolescents. In fact, many young adult books have been the basis for prime-time movies. Unfortunately, it is frequently not clear that the made-for-TV movies are based on books. In fact, the name of the author and the title of the book from which the script was adapted are often hidden in the credits. And since many films do not have the same name as the book, discovering which TV movies are based on books is nearly impossible.

The Public Broadcasting System (PBS) has many series based on children's, young adult, and classic books. Some of these are produced as part of a regular, ongoing series (such as "All Creatures Great and Small" from the books of James Herriot) or single shows based on individual books. "Masterpiece Theatre" is known for its literary presentation of classic works, and "Wonderworks" presents programming based on children's and young adult books of high quality. If parents watch these shows with their adolescents, they can encourage them to read the books on which the shows are based. If parents read the books too, many worthwhile discussions can result. Many schools and libraries receive free information and teaching guides on these programs, which they may be willing to share with interested parents.

News and Documentaries

News programs and documentaries are useful for obtaining a quick overview of a subject or issue. Adolescents who are encouraged to watch appropriate programs of this type often develop an interest in the subject or issue discussed. I have a friend whose professional interest in aquatic biology grew from watching Jacques Cousteau underwater exploration programs. Many programs of this type recommend additional reading. Sometimes transcripts of the programs that include bibliographies are available for a small charge.

How to Make Television Work for Your Family

- Limit the number of hours television is watched.
- Encourage selective viewing.
- Plan weekly TV viewing by selecting programs carefully. (Consult television listings for help in planning your viewing.)
- Seek information from libraries or schools about shows of educational value or book tie-ins.
- Seek shows of high quality and high entertainment value.
- Obtain books related to the shows you plan to watch. (Some school and public libraries do weekly or monthly displays of books related to television programs.)
- If possible, read the book prior to watching the show.
- Recommend appropriate books to adolescents.
- Try to watch shows as a family and discuss them afterwards.
- If you watch quiz shows, watch those with educational value. Play along with contestants.
- Allow adolescents to select some popular television shows. Keep in mind how essential peer acceptance is to adoles-

cents. Watch these shows with them and discuss the issues involved.

- Sporting events can lead to good reading. Check your public library for books about sports.
- Check for presentations of high-quality motion pictures, particularly on cable stations.
- Watch for details in the program: Is it shot on location? Is the setting appropriate? Are the props appropriate for the time or location? If you have read the book, do you agree with the way characters are portrayed? How does the script differ from the book? Be a critical viewer and encourage the adolescent to be the same.
- Examine news programs for bias. Are all sides of an issue presented? How much time is given to a particular story? Does the report appear to be accurate? Do the pictures go along with the account? Are sources given? Are they reliable?
- Avoid having the television on as a background noise. Avoid watching it during dinner. Don't use it as a substitute for real communication.
- Be a model television viewer. If you watch six to eight hours of television a day, your adolescent will probably do the same.

Subscription Television and Videocassettes

Cable television, subscription TV, and videocassettes have changed the way Americans watch television. Television shows can be recorded and watched at another time. Families who have a VCR or subscribe to cable television can view recent motion pictures at home. These new technologies give families more flexibility in terms of viewing choice and time.

Favorite television programs can be recorded, then watched together at a time convenient for the entire family. You might choose to record a program at the same time you are watching another program on a different channel. Both of these practices have the danger of increasing the number of hours of television viewing. However, if families are selective, these practices can broaden the scope of viewing possibilities.

Many families are discovering that renting movies on video-cassette increases viewing options. Parents can select films of interest to the entire family. Many films are wonderful entertainment and serve as discussion starters that can lead to new reading interests or open channels of communication between parents and adolescents. The American Library Association publishes two good sources for helping parents select appropriate videos and films for adolescents: "Selected Films for Young Adults" and "Selected Videos and Films for Young Adults" (ALA, Young Adult Library Services Association, 50 East Huron Street, Chicago, Illinois 60611).

Paid subscription television also broadens the range of television viewing. New networks featuring sports, news, and religious programming are available in many areas. As with videocassettes, this broad range of choice can have a positive effect on family viewing. Parents need to teach adolescents to select their viewing carefully.

. . . . . .

Motion Pictures and Movie Theaters

Attending popular films has been an important social event for adolescents for several generations. The motion picture industry has capitalized on—and, some people believe, exploited—the large number of adolescent consumers. It has become increasingly difficult for parents to control the films seen by adolescents. In generations past, parents of preadolescents and early adolescents could often influence movie viewing by driving adolescents only to theaters showing films of which the parents approved.

Today, however, most movie theaters show more than one feature film, and some show as many as five or eight at a time. Once in the theater, the young person can select the film she or he wants to see. Therefore, it is now more important than ever for parents to communicate with adolescents about the films they see.

How to Make Films Work for Your Family

- Preview film choices with the adolescent in local newspaper listings. Suggest that some choices are better than others and explain why without being judgmental.
- Encourage the adolescent to read and listen to reviews of the films.
- Make a regular habit of discussing films with the adolescent, even those you have not seen. You might ask, "Is this a film I should go see?"
- Encourage the adolescent to see films that will do more than entertain. Try to broaden the adolescent's film-viewing menu and maturity.
- If you rent or purchase videocassette films, view them as a family and talk about them afterward using book discussion techniques suggested in chapter 5.
- When appropriate go to the movies with the adolescent and encourage discussion afterward.
- Broaden the discussion to include elements important to the media of film: camera angle, editing, acting, action sequences, script, etc.
- Encourage the adolescent to read the book on which the film was based, if there is one. Or, if possible, suggest the adolescent read the book before seeing the film.
- Discuss with the adolescent the differences between the book and the film. Which did the adolescent like better? How were the two media different? What choices might the ado-

lescent have made if she or he were the script writer or director?

- Offer your opinions if you have seen the film, but avoid being judgmental of the adolescent's opinions.

· · · · · ·

The Computer as a Literacy Aid

Many adolescents are familiar with computers used both as an entertainment option and as an educational tool. Large numbers of adolescents have personal or family computers on which they play computer games. Others go to malls or video arcades to play sophisticated computer games. An increasing number of adolescents actively participate in computer networks in which they communicate with other users. Likewise, many schools have computers and an increasing number of students use software programs for educational purposes and learn word processing skills. An interest in computers can lead adolescents to many magazines and books on computing, computer games, and various aspects of computer technology. Some adolescents decide on their own to move from playing games on the computer to learning more about how the computer works. Others need to be encouraged by parents.

How to Make Computers Work for Your Family

- If you do not have a family personal computer, consider purchasing one. Many excellent used personal computers can be purchased. Ask around and check your local newspaper. Don't buy a used computer unless the manuals are available, you have tested the hardware, and it can be upgraded to meet your needs.
- Make the purchase of the computer a family project. If the

adolescent is earning money, he or she might help contribute to the purchase of the computer or its software.

- Discuss with the adolescent which computers might be appropriate to purchase. If possible, purchase a computer that is compatible with those available at school, and purchase software, such as word processing programs, that your adolescent can use on the computer at school.

- Ask the media adviser at the school what computer and software she or he would suggest.

- Once the computer has been purchased and installed, learn how to use it as a family. Many community colleges offer free or inexpensive courses that you and your adolescent can take together. Purchase magazines and books about using your computer.

- Read and discuss the books together. Investigate with the adolescent appropriate and useful software.

- If the adolescent does not know how to type, encourage her or him to take typing at school or enroll the adolescent in a typing course. Lack of typing skill limits one's ability to use the computer.

- Encourage the adolescent to use the computer for more than playing games. Suggest typing school papers on the computer. Examine various interactive reading and writing programs.

- Monitor the adolescent's use of the computer: Is too much time being spent on games? If the adolescent is participating in a computer network, is it appropriate and safe?

- Be cautious when purchasing computer software for adolescents; many computer games are too mature. Some video stores rate computer software by maturity (similar to movie ratings), and most have a liberal return policy. If your video store does not have a rating system, ask the clerk to recommend an appropriate computer review magazine. If neither a rating system nor rating magazines are available, find another source for purchasing the software.

- Discuss with the adolescent how she or he is using the computer. Ask the adolescent to teach you to play the games and show you the network.

- Do not hesitate to limit the adolescent's non-education-related time on the computer.

Computers Can Encourage Reading and Writing

Computers offer many possibilities for reading beyond books and magazines about computers. An exciting new trend in computer software is computer fiction. Text-based, interactive fiction is available from at least a dozen companies for almost every type of computer. The fiction is interactive in that readers not only read the story but interact with it by using the keyboard. For example, readers can alter the plot of the story to determine what will happen next. The story proceeds based on readers' responses. In most text-based software, readers are not limited to three or four choices but can type almost anything that logically fits the storyline and character development. The only limitation is that the programmer must have anticipated the readers' instructions.

Most of the plots currently available are adventure, fantasy, or science fiction. The stories take on the characteristics of a game as readers attempt to extricate the hero from various situations. Many of the stories are based on fiction available in traditional book form. Adolescents who become fascinated with a particular program will probably want to read the book on which it is based. Some of these stories have been adapted for the computer by the authors of the original books, others by computer programmers, and still others by writers who are hired to turn the books into computer adventure games. Consequently, many of the programs are true to their literary form. Readers must comprehend the author's literary techniques in order to do well in the game. They are rewarded in the program for selecting options that are appropriate to the characters and the plot.

Interactive fiction is not true literature, but it does use literary techniques and requires the reader's involvement in the story. Adolescents' active involvement in computer fiction may transfer to their reading and writing. Since active involvement with the characters and plot is necessary to comprehend a traditional piece of fiction, the skills learned in playing the game may help readers improve their ability to comprehend what they read. Likewise, computer fiction can help adolescents understand literary techniques used by writers; for example, writers must remain consistent in the development of characters.

Interactive computer fiction is a relatively recent phenomenon. It is still being perfected. The best programs allow almost unlimited choice. Programs that are more literary are better than those that are simply games. The more literary the program, the more likely it is to use techniques adolescents will need when they read a novel or short story, and the more likely it is to encourage the adolescent to read the book on which it is based.

The programs contain varying amounts of graphic representation. Though the graphic representation is not essential to the game, it does make it more interesting for many adolescents. It is important that graphics be faithful to the plot, characters, and setting. Programs with limited graphics have a greater potential to help adolescents develop their own imaginations. As in books without illustrations, young readers must imagine the characters and settings when they are not provided by program graphics.

Parents of adolescents who are interested in computers may find these programs a useful way to move adolescents from the keyboard to books. Most computers and software programs, however, are considerably more expensive than books. Because of their price and varying quality, it is important that parents examine the programs carefully for their literary quality, number of options, and potential to move adolescents into books.

I have many concerns about the negative effect of the electronic media on adolescents, but I've come to realize that these concerns come from misuse of the media rather than the media themselves. Used effectively, TV and film can be marvelous entertainment and educational tools. They can lead adolescents to books. The same is true of computers.

We have a responsibility to teach young people to use electronic media to their benefit. We must encourage adolescents to understand the potential advantages and disadvantages of TV, movies, and computers, and they will come to appreciate them more.

THREE

. . . .

Locating Books

7

. . . .

Selecting Books

I believe that [adolescents] are better judges of what constitutes a "good" book than adults. [They] care nothing about best-seller lists, what book has won an award and which one has not. [They] know what they like and they read it—not once, but a half dozen times or more.
Jeannette H. Eyerly

Selecting Books for Adolescents

Selecting books can be difficult. How many times have you gone to a bookstore or library planning to buy or borrow a book and come away empty-handed? Sometimes there are too many books to choose from and not enough time to explore them thoroughly; sometimes nothing looks interesting.

Avid adult readers find ways to deal with the problem of too much or too little to read. We have many selection techniques. We may ask advice from friends, librarians, or salespeople in bookstores. Some people read book reviews in newspapers or magazines. Others belong to book clubs. We may read everything we can find by a favorite author or in a favorite genre. Avid adult readers find ways to locate books they are likely to enjoy.

Adolescents often have not developed these skills, so they may select inappropriate books. Teenagers who are unable to find books they enjoy sometimes quit reading. Some adolescents become stuck in a particular kind of book or in books by a particular author because they have not discovered appealing alternatives. This frequently happens to adolescents who are initially captivated by series books but come to find them less and less appealing and don't know how to locate other books of interest. Adolescents stuck in a reading rut usually become bored and read less.

Required Reading Can Be Counterproductive

We like to think that adolescents develop reading interest in school, and some do. But since adolescents may not enjoy the books they are assigned to read, required reading does little to build reading interest. If students are permitted to select books to read, they may not be given any guidance in how to select books. Even if they do receive guidance, it may not be helpful. For example, some high school teachers would like all of their students to read the classics, but many young readers are not developmentally ready to read the classics and cannot see themselves on the pages of the book. Even if they are willing to read a required book, requiring specific books does not help them find books on their own for pleasure reading.

When teachers provide adolescents with reading choices, there is sometimes not enough help in learning how to make the choice. Recently a teenage friend called to ask my advice. She is currently enrolled in a freshman honors English class. She had been assigned a year-long project to read six books by the same author and then lead a seminar about the books with her fellow students. However, she had no idea which author to select. She is an avid reader, so she had in mind some authors that she liked, but she had no idea if any of them had written six books. She went to her high school library, but she couldn't find six books by any author with whom she was familiar. My adolescent friend was very frustrated. Although she had been attempting conscientiously to complete her assignment, she had been unable to do so. Her teacher had not suggested resources for locating either the author or the books written by the author. I first suggested to her that she check the names of several authors she liked in *Books in Print* to see if there were six books currently available by one or more of these authors. She explained that she had to give the name of the author to the teacher the next day and had no time to go to the library prior to her first-period English class. So I asked, "Who are the authors you enjoy?" She rattled off four or five names. I told her which ones had published at least six books and also suggested some alternative authors she might like. I wondered how she would have completed her assignment if she hadn't had someone to help her locate an appropriate author.

Parents Can Help

If adolescents are unable to learn to select books on their own, they will not develop into mature readers. In fact, even good readers may quit reading. Parents must become involved in adolescents' book selections. The first step is knowing which books adolescents will enjoy.

If adolescents have not yet developed the ability to select books on their own, parents can help by selecting books for them. However, the vast number of available books can frustrate us. Reading the books, visiting the library to keep up with new acquisitions, or checking bookstores on a regular basis is too time consuming for most parents, so we must use some of the same tools we use in selecting books for ourselves. The following guidelines may help.

A Guide to Selecting Books for Adolescents

- Using the book lists in chapters 11 and 12 as a guide, check local bookstores and libraries to determine the best source of books.
- Keep in mind your adolescent's interests, favorite television shows or movies, and the kinds of books he or she has enjoyed in the past.
- Examine books to determine if your adolescent will find them interesting (see chapter 10).
- Make an honest evaluation of how well your teenager reads.
- Ask a young adult librarian, a knowledgeable bookstore clerk, or a teacher for help in selecting books.
- Ask your child's friends what they are reading.
- Enroll your adolescent in a young adult book club. Check with the school to see if any are available through his or her classes.
- Examine books to determine if they are too hard or too easy. (As a rule, easier books have shorter sentences, words, paragraphs, and chapters.)
- Estimate the age of the main character in the book. Most adolescents prefer books with characters slightly older than they are.
- Select three very different books to borrow from the library. They should all be books your adolescent is capable of reading, that deal with his or her interests, and that are like books he or she has selected in the past. Then ask your adolescent to choose a favorite.
- Avoid falling into the trap of saying, "This is a book I would have liked at your age."
- Respect your youngster's choice from the books you selected. Use this choice to guide you in selecting or purchasing the next book.

- As time goes on, select *slightly* more demanding books of higher literary quality.
- In time, select books within parallel genres. (For example, if the teenager likes romances, move to historical romance.)
- Don't push; be patient.
- Encourage your adolescent to select books without your help.

. . . . . .

Encouraging Self-Selection

Eventually, selecting books for adolescents becomes counterproductive. They may begin to rely on parents' selections and fail to develop their own selection skills. To avoid this, we must help adolescents become confident in their ability to select books. This confidence is central to becoming a mature reader.

A Guide to Helping Adolescents Select Their Own Books

- Make sure adolescents visit the public library and bookstores regularly.
- Be sure the library and bookstores visited are ones in which adolescents are treated with respect. For example, if the young adult section of your public library is in the children's room, adolescents may be embarrassed to be seen there. Express your concern about this to the head of the library.
- Be sure adolescents know where they can find appropriate books in the library or bookstore. (Don't lead your teenager to the location; just be specific in explaining where to find the books.)
- Discuss with adolescents the best bookstores for finding good young adult books.

- Introduce adolescents to librarians and bookstore clerks who know young adult books.
- When you and your adolescent are with her or his friends, ask them about the books they read and enjoy.
- Encourage adolescents to purchase books from school book fairs and school book clubs and to join a young adult book club. (See chapter 9 for more information.)
- Purchase an annotated bibliography for your adolescents and share chapters 11 and 12 of this book with them. Encourage them to use these sources in making selections.
- Discuss books of all kinds with the adolescent. (See chapter 5 for discussion hints.)
- Suggest books or authors you think adolescents might enjoy.
- Respect your adolescent's choices.

Annotated Books and Book Lists

Three valuable reference books published by the National Council of Teachers of English (1111 Kenyon Road, Urbana, Illinois 61801) help adolescents select their own books. *Books for You*, compiled for high school students to use on their own, is also a useful source for parents. More than one thousand books of high literary quality and of interest to teenage readers are annotated. *Your Reading*, designed to be used by middle and junior high school students, annotates more than one thousand books published within a two-year period. *High Interest–Easy Reading* is particularly valuable for parents of reluctant readers. It suggests more than four hundred books for adolescents who have difficulty reading. The books selected are designed to appeal to the maturity of the adolescent while not frustrating them by being too difficult to comprehend. All of these reference guides are frequently revised and are available at low cost.

Many organizations update and publish reading lists of books for young adults. These lists usually annotate twenty to thirty recently published books recommended for adolescents and are available free or for a small charge. Most of the organizations require that you include with your request a stamped, self-addressed envelope. Several lists—"Best Books for Young Adults"; "Newbery Medal Books"; "Outstanding Books for the College Bound: Biographies, Fiction, Fine Arts, Nonfiction and Theatre" (five lists); "Margaret A. Edwards Award Authors for Outstanding Literature for Young Adults"; "Coretta Scott King Award and Honor Books"; and "The Mildred L. Batchelder Award Books" (young adult books translated into English)—are all available from the Young Adult Library Services Association, American Library Association, 50 East Huron Street, Chicago, Illinois 60611. "Books for the Teenager" is available from The New York Public Library, Office of Branch Libraries, 455 Fifth Avenue, New York, New York 10016. Another excellent resource is the *Interracial Books for Children Bulletin* published by the Council on Interracial Books (1841 Broadway, New York, New York 10023).

In addition, the International Reading Association (Box 8139, Newark, Delaware 19714) publishes "Young Adults' Choices," an annotated book list that is updated annually. Books on the list are selected by teenage readers. Single copies are free, but requests must include a self-addressed envelope stamped with two ounces of first-class postage.

Parents should also check public libraries for books about books. Librarians can suggest annotated book lists to help parents locate all kinds of books appropriate for adolescents, including multicultural books, books for reluctant readers, books for readers with handicaps, books for readers experiencing difficult social or personal problems, et cetera.

. . . . . .

Selecting Magazines for Adolescents

Adolescents are consumers of magazines. Nearly every year, often more than once a year, a new teen-oriented periodical appears in bookstores and other markets. Some magazines, written for and by adolescents, are very good. Unfortunately, others tend to exploit teenagers through both their articles and their advertising. It is important that parents help adolescents select those magazines that will not only appeal to them, but will help them learn and mature.

A Guide to Helping Adolescents
Select Their Own Magazines

Alice Denham suggests that the following are important in evaluating a teen-oriented magazine:

- *Format:* The cover should be colorful and accurately represent the contents of the magazine. The table of contents should be easy to find and to use. Page makeup and design should be attractive. Subject matter in articles should look appealing. Pictures should be clear, related to articles, and placed in appropriate places within articles.
- *Readability and Interest Level:* The subject matter should relate to the adolescent's interests, needs, and intellectual and emotional maturity. Writing should be quickly paced and engaging. Reading level (vocabulary and sentence structure) should be appropriate for the adolescent. Technical vocabulary should be carefully defined in the context of the article.
- *Advertising:* Advertising should be clearly identified as advertising, not disguised as articles. Products should be appealing to teenagers and accessible for their consumption; they should not be harmful to adolescents. The advertising

should be balanced with content—as a rule of thumb, advertisements should comprise no more than 50 percent of a magazine's contents.

- *Content:* A variety of content is desirable: fiction, nonfiction, features on adolescents, items of interest to teens (articles about education, employment, volunteer service, sports and athletes, clothing, dating, movie and television reviews, book reviews, et cetera), articles written by adolescents, unbiased reporting on current issues important to teenagers (abortion, birth control, working, smoking, drugs, teen pregnancy, environmental issues, et cetera). Articles should be accurate and authors should have knowledge of the topic.

- *Values:* According to Denham, "Values are infused in any magazine both covertly and overtly." Values can be suggested subtly by the content of articles, for example: making oneself beautiful for the opposite sex, portrayal of men and women only in certain occupations, the importance of sports over other pursuits, reviewing books of interest to adolescents, et cetera. She suggests that adults help teens seek magazines that overtly suggest positive values such as these following:

- Interpersonal relationships. Honesty and responsibility in relationships; acknowledgment that relationships require understanding and effort; understanding that not all relationships are positive.

- Sexual relationships. Responsibility in mature intimate relationships and their impact on the individuals involved.

- Adult-teen relationships. Building mutual respect between teens and parents, teachers, and other adults.

- Self-image. Growth of adolescent's personality; feeling good about oneself; determining (and doing) what is right.

- Intellect. Nurturing and developing one's own intelligence; commitment to schooling and reading.

- Health. Encouragement of exercise, fitness, good nutrition, and encouragement of healthful living and avoidance of dangerous substances.
- Work ethic. Illustrations of ways to become productive in school, the community, and employment.
- Citizenship. Unbiased reporting on issues important to adolescents; encouraging active involvement in school and community.
- Ecology. Understanding interrelationships of humans and wildlife; protection of environment.

The best way to assist adolescents in selecting reading material is to be a model. As adolescents observe the selection procedures of influential adults they begin to transfer the techniques to their own book selection.

Like adult readers, young adults usually act on reading suggestions from their friends, but parents and teachers are also influential.

The best way to be a valuable resource in the reading selections of adolescents is by knowing what they will enjoy reading. We can do this by being aware of their reading interests and matching these interests to books at appropriate reading levels. It is essential that we assist adolescents in learning to select their own books and magazines by developing an environment in which reading and books are central.

The task is not easy, but our influence and guidance may help adolescents become mature readers who can appreciate fine literature.

8

· ·

Borrowing Books

Read . . . and you will discover a new world of wonder where librarians will provide you with the magic key to the best friends you could ever have—books.   Lee Hadley and Ann Irwin

Why Borrow Books?

The only way to become a reader is to read books and other materials that meet many needs and address many interests. Adolescents need books to read for pleasure, informational sources to provide material for research projects, magazines to help keep their knowledge and interests current, dictionaries and almanacs, newspapers, and many other types of reading materials.

One of our major responsibilities as parents is to provide an environment in which books are plentiful, but purchasing the vast array of books required by adolescents is impossible. Many books must be borrowed from libraries.

Using the Public Library

Public libraries allow everyone to borrow books, films, audio- and videocassettes, magazines, and other materials. Unfortunately, many people do not take advantage of this free resource.

Almost every town has a public library. Most libraries have separate sections for children and many have separate sections for adolescents. If there is no public library in your area, there are probably other sources from which to borrow books. Bookmobiles visit smaller communities on a regular basis. Many small communities have branch libraries or reading rooms from which readers can borrow books. If you are unsure whether these services exist in your area, you can call the nearest public library and ask how it serves your community.

Services for Adolescents

Many libraries have special rooms or sections for children's books. Because adolescents are uncomfortable using the children's room and have difficulty locating appropriate books in the adult book section, many libraries also have rooms or sections for young adults. Often, there is an overlap in material housed in the children's and in the young adult's book sections of the library, but usually material in children's rooms goes through upper elementary school level and material for young adults begins at middle school level.

The best sections for young adults have comfortable areas for pleasure reading, tables for quiet discussion, and carrels for independent study. They are decorated with posters, pictures, and books of interest to adolescents.

Many libraries have special programs for adolescents. Some have regular newsletters that list special events such as movies, visits by authors, plays, storytelling sessions, book discussion groups, and writing circles. Diane P. Tuccillo, a young adult librarian at the Mesa, Arizona, public library, cites some of the programs of the young adult services department of her library, which other libraries might offer as well:

- *Booktalking:* A booktalk is a sort of commercial about a book. Librarians meet with small groups of adolescents to tell them about books they might enjoy. Many public libraries not only provide booktalk services in the library, but also send librarians to schools and service organizations.
- *Storytelling Program:* Some public libraries have storytelling programs for teenagers. Like booktalking programs, these are typically offered in the library, schools, churches, and various service organizations.
- *Young Adult Advisory Councils:* Some public libraries have advisory councils made up of young adults. These councils meet monthly or bimonthly to review books and films and plan library activities for adolescents. Some publish newsletters that are distributed to schools and parents and provide information about what is new for adolescents in the public library.
- *Magazines:* Some large public libraries publish magazines of writing by and for young adults. The Mesa library, for example, has an annual magazine that publishes young adult science fiction and fantasy art and writing by or for young adults. Schools and individual adolescents are encouraged to submit articles, poems, short stories, and art work to the publication, which also includes information about library services for adolescents. Young adults serve on the editorial board of this magazine.
- *Tours:* Most public libraries provide tours for groups of young adults. These tours focus on all library services of interest to adolescents and often feature booktalks or storytelling sessions.
- *New Books/Professional Journals/Sourcebooks on Literature:* Tuccillo points out that most large public libraries have larger materials budgets than school libraries. Therefore, the collec-

tion of young adult books and related journals and source-
books is frequently more extensive. Public young adult
librarians can provide information to adolescents, parents,
and teachers about the material available in the public
library.

- *Newsletters:* Young adult departments of public libraries often publish newsletters about new books, programs, and
services. These newsletters are frequently available free of
charge to teachers, school librarians, and friends of the library. Parents and adolescents can often pick up copies of
newsletters at the checkout desk of the young adult room.
- *Special Cooperative Projects:* Many public libraries have special community projects. The Des Moines, Iowa, public library, for example, has a project called "Reading and
Sharing" in which teenagers read and discuss books with
younger children during the summer vacation. The West-
chester County, New York, public library has sponsored a
program designed to promote reading among learning disa-
bled students by promoting a partnership between the home,
the school, and the public library.

In addition, many librarians compile annotated bibliographies
on specific topics for parents, adolescents, and teachers. These
include summaries of books, reading and interest levels, publication information, and other helpful information. Parents should
ask if their public libraries have any of these services. If not, it
may be possible to encourage the library to establish such resources by volunteering your help to get them started. Unfortunately, even large public libraries have been forced to limit some
services in recent years as tax support has diminished in many
states. Most libraries have chosen to limit services, even operating
hours, rather than cut book and materials budgets.

All public libraries have reference sections from which books typically cannot be borrowed but provide adolescents with quick access to large amounts of information. Reference sections usually include encyclopedias, dictionaries, atlases, indexes to magazine and newspaper articles, government documents, telephone books, geological surveys and maps, and almanacs.

Most libraries have current magazines and newspapers. The typical library subscribes to several dozen magazines for readers of various ages with varied interests and backgrounds. Many also subscribe to specialized magazines in addition to the local newspaper, a daily paper from the nearest large city, *The New York Times, The Wall Street Journal*, and papers from several other large cities. Most large and middle-sized libraries keep back issues of major papers and some magazines on microfilm or microfiche. Back issues of magazines or newspapers the library does not receive may be available through interlibrary loan (a computerized system through which one public library can borrow material from another public library), or the library may be willing to purchase them for its collection.

In addition, many public libraries lend records, recordings, slides, filmstrips, movies, videocassettes, artwork, toys, and other educational items.

Most public libraries are part of state library systems and have access to services of libraries throughout the state. Computerization has made it easy for librarians to locate books and information not housed in the local library but available through interlibrary loan.

Teaching Young People to Use Libraries

A family visit to the public library is a good way to help all family members become familiar with library services. Because most libraries offer tours to small groups, parents may want to encourage organizations to which the adolescent belongs to sponsor a tour of the public library. Getting library cards is simple. Usually the only thing required is residency in the area the library serves. Even nonresidents can borrow from most libraries by paying a small fee. Most public libraries require adults to sign for cards obtained by minors.

Few schools take students to the public library, so it is up to parents to teach youngsters to use the public library. Adolescents need to know where reference materials are kept, how magazines are shelved and referenced, how to use the card catalog or the computer catalog to find books in the library, where to find books and how to check them out, where to find nonfiction offerings, and which librarian to ask for help. Most adolescents have difficulty locating material in public libraries because they do not know where and how to find it and are unwilling to ask. Once they learn how to use the library, they are likely to use it often.

. . . . . .

Using School Libraries

Studies show that schools that spend the most money on their libraries are likely to have students who score higher on standardized achievement tests and college entrance exams. Because schools are aware of these studies, they strive to make their libraries useful and inviting places. Most schools train their students to use the library.

Because libraries are so important to adolescents' education and reading development, parents may want to use the following checklist to determine if the school library is adequate to meet students' personal and academic needs.

A Checklist of Middle and Junior High School Library Services

A middle or junior high school library should ideally have the following things:

- A wide variety of fiction books (children's, young adult, adult) appropriate for all readers in the school.
- A wide variety of nonfiction books allowing all readers in the school to research a variety of topics.
- A large number of paperbacks for young adults, shelved separately for browsing and borrowing.
- At least three complete sets of encyclopedias.
- Several intermediate, advanced, and adult dictionaries from different publishers.
- Several atlases.
- Several current almanacs, including special interest almanacs (such as sports).
- A wide variety of magazines of interest to the age group (*Teen, Boys' Life*).
- A wide variety of adult general interest magazines (*Sports Illustrated, Time*).
- Several special interest magazines appropriate for research projects (*Smithsonian, American Heritage, National Geographic*).
- Open shelves for current magazines.
- Several years of back issues of magazines most useful in research.
- Easy access to all books and magazines for all students.
- Easily accessible indexes of magazines available in the library.
- A professional library for teachers.
- Several copies of the local newspaper and at least one state and two national newspapers.
- Adequate and comfortable seating for a full class of students.
- Adequate space for individual study and research.
- Displays that make students want to read and learn.
- A policy that encourages students to use the library.

- Good lighting and ventilation.
- A friendly, helpful, and knowledgeable librarian.

High school libraries should contain materials to help students gain the skills to compete in college-level work. The following checklist can help parents determine if the high school library's materials, facilities, and services are adequate for adolescents' personal and academic needs.

A Checklist of High School Library Services

A high school library should ideally have the following things:

- A wide variety of fiction (young adult, adult and classic) appropriate for poor to gifted readers.
- A wide variety of nonfiction, written by knowledgeable researchers, in all subject areas taught within the school, on a wide range of reading levels.
- At least four complete sets of encyclopedias from different publishers.
- Many different intermediate, advanced, and adult dictionaries.
- Numerous atlases on all areas of the world.
- Many almanacs, including special interest almanacs.
- A wide variety of reference books about jobs, colleges, authors, historical data, and scientific data.
- College catalogs.
- Open shelves of magazines of interest to teens (*Seventeen, Hot Rod*).
- Open shelves of current general interest adult magazines, including those for advanced readers (*The New Yorker, Harper's*).
- Open shelves for current specialized magazines (*Scientific American, Psychology Today*).

- Several copies of the local newspaper and at least two state and three national newspapers.
- At least five years of bound volumes (or microfiche) of magazines important to research in subject areas taught within the school.
- Appropriate indexes for easy access to articles in magazines.
- Easy access to all books, reference materials, and magazines.
- A large selection of paperbacks for both young and older adolescents, shelved separately for browsing and borrowing.
- A professional section, including books and journals for teachers in all subject areas.
- Adequate and comfortable seating for a full class of students.
- Quiet areas for individual study and research.
- Tables for quiet conversation.
- Access, through cataloging and appropriate equipment, to audiovisual material and computer software.
- Audiovisuals (videos, records, cassette tapes) appropriate to the curriculum and places for individuals and small groups to view or listen to them.
- Computer software appropriate to the curriculum that can either be used in the library or checked out for student use.
- Displays that make students want to read and learn.
- A policy that encourages active use of the library.
- Good lighting and ventilation.
- Friendly, helpful, and knowledgeable librarians and staff.

How to Assess a School Library

Parents can use one of these checklists to assess school libraries. Often the best approach is to discuss the library's strengths and weaknesses with a librarian. Many schools have established parent groups or committees for this purpose.

Of course, not all libraries have all the attributes listed, and many have more. The best-equipped school libraries have easily accessible video and audio equipment, computers, and software, and separate rooms for small class meetings or group study. However, many smaller school libraries have decided to limit purchase of expensive equipment so that they can utilize their limited budgets to purchase books and other written material. In an era in which many parents have more choice about the school in which to enroll their children, one important way to assess the quality of a school is to examine the strengths of its library.

Another aspect of libraries—the people who work in them—can be hard for parents to assess. A dedicated, knowledgeable, caring librarian can make a good library even better and help to overcome the shortcomings of a poorer library. However, school libraries are often understaffed. In addition, school librarians are expected to be audiovisual experts, book and audiovisual material purchasers, computer technologists, surrogate teachers, and disciplinarians. The time they can spend with individuals may be limited. School libraries with good volunteer programs can often limit the problems of the overworked school librarian. Today, many schools have excellent volunteer programs for adults who assist the librarian with paperwork and help individuals or small groups of students access books and important reference materials.

The ability to use and enjoy libraries can change adolescents' lives. In libraries teenagers can discover the world of books and equip themselves to compete in education and the adult marketplace. With access to reading materials from public and school libraries, home reading shelves need never be bare.

9

· ·

Buying Books

*Our goal as writers for [and parents of] the . . . young is of course
to make them inveterate, chronic readers whose tastes keep pace
with their maturity.*

Richard Peck

Building a Home Library

The importance of a home library to the development of a lifelong reading habit cannot be overemphasized. Children who live
with books and who watch their parents select and read books
from a home library are likely to become adults who read. A
publication of the Childrens' Book Council, *CBC Features*, has a
regular column, "Books Remembered," in which well-known
children's and young adult authors talk about how they became
readers and writers. In one issue, British writer Rosemary Wells
described how both her parents' and grandparents' homes were
filled with books that reflected their personalities and interests.
From reading in her grandparents' home each Sunday as a child
she developed a love of history and politics. From her mother she
learned to love books about art and all things British. Is it any
wonder that she became a writer of British historical fiction for
young adults?

What Books Are Essential to a Home Library?

The wider the variety of books, the wider the reading interests adolescents are likely to develop. Therefore, it is important that home libraries contain a wide variety of fiction and nonfiction appropriate to the needs, interests, and maturity of all family members. Books should be available throughout the house: cookbooks in the kitchen; nonfiction in the den, study, or living room; favorite fiction books in bedrooms. Even bathrooms and workshops are appropriate places for books.

If preschoolers have bookshelves in their bedrooms, their libraries are likely to grow and mature with them. Favorite books are retained and more mature books are added. It is important for parents to ensure that this book collection continues and grows into adolescence.

As young people reach preadolescence, their libraries should begin to contain essential reference books. There are some books every home library should have.

Dictionary. Most homes have dictionaries, but some dictionaries are particularly appropriate for adolescents. The best adult dictionary is too complicated when a teenager says "How can I look it up if I can't spell it?" or "I can never understand the definition."

There are three categories of dictionaries appropriate for the stages of adolescent intellectual development: intermediate dictionaries for preadolescents (ages 10–13), advanced or student dictionaries for early adolescents (ages 13–15), and adult or college dictionaries for late adolescents (ages 15–18). Intermediate dictionaries contain most words preadolescents need and use. Typically, they have about one-third of the entries of adult dictionaries, list fewer definitions per word, use illustrations, are written on a reading level appropriate to the user, and divide words into syllables without giving specific etymologies. Many intermediate dictionaries contain sample sentences to help users understand words. In short, they are easier to use and understand and less intimidating than adult dictionaries.

Advanced or student dictionaries contain words most commonly used by junior and senior high school students. Like intermediate dictionaries, they are easier to use than their adult counterparts. However, they are more complete and adult appearing than intermediate dictionaries. They provide a transition between intermediate and adult dictionaries. Several good intermediate and advanced dictionaries are available.

- *Macmillan Dictionary for Students* (grades 6–11). Macmillan, 1984.
- *Webster's High School Dictionary*. Merriam-Webster, 1990.
- *Webster's Intermediate Dictionary* (grades 9–12). Merriam-Webster, 1986.
- *Webster's Scholastic Dictionary* (grades 9–12). Airmont, paper.
- *Webster's New World Dictionary: Student Edition* (grades 4–8). Simon & Schuster, 1980.
- *Webster's New World Dictionary for Young Readers*. Merriam-Webster, 1989.
- *Webster's New World Dictionary for Young Adults*. Simon & Schuster, 1992.
- *Webster's School Dictionary* (grades 8–12). Merriam-Webster, 1980.

Parents should plan to replace dictionaries every three or four years. By the time adolescents enter high school most are ready to use adult dictionaries to supplement easier intermediate or advanced dictionaries. Though the adult dictionary is not likely to replace intermediate or advanced dictionaries until late in high school, adolescents should have access to a recent edition of an

adult dictionary. The following checklist will help you purchase
the appropriate dictionary.

A CHECKLIST FOR PURCHASING A
DICTIONARY FOR ADOLESCENTS

- The adolescent will be able to locate words efficiently in this
  dictionary.
- The adolescent will be able to understand the definitions.
- The print is readable.
- The illustrations or sample sentences make definitions easy
  to understand.
- The information is neither too complex nor too elementary.
- A pronunciation key, functional labels, inflectional forms,
  cross-references, synonyms, and abbreviations are included.
- The number of words included is adequate for the adolescent's educational needs.
- The aids at the front and back of the dictionary are appropriate for the adolescent's educational and personal needs
  (spelling rules, forms of address, name pronunciations and
  derivations, capitals and their states and countries, and punc-
  tuation rules).

An interesting supplemental dictionary that can be very helpful
to adolescents who often use the incorrect word is *Word Traps:
A Dictionary of the 7000 Most Confusing Sound-Alike and Look-
Alike Words*, by Jordan Linfield and Joseph Krevisky (Macmillan/
Collier, 1993). This book is a great resource for the whole family.

Thesaurus. A good thesaurus for young adults provides them
with carefully selected synonyms for words they use. In addition,
a good thesaurus specifically designed for adolescents gives sample sentences to illustrate appropriate use of the word. A good
thesaurus also contains identification of parts of speech and an-
tonyms (opposites) of words. *The Facts on File Student's Thesau-*

rus, edited by Paul Hellweg, is a particularly appropriate choice for pre- and early adolescents. Another, more complete thesaurus appropriate for older adolescents is *The Random House Thesaurus: College Edition*.

Encyclopedia. An encyclopedia is an expensive but valuable family investment. An encyclopedia is an excellent beginning place for research and gives adolescents the opportunity to explore many topics. There are several junior encyclopedias appropriate for pre- and early adolescents, which differ from adult encyclopedias in their presentation of information. They tend to be more colorful, contain more pictures, use simple vocabulary and conversational tone, encourage additional investigation, and pose thought-provoking questions. Just as with dictionaries, adult encyclopedias may be difficult to use and not helpful to adolescents. Younger adolescents find the descriptions complex and the cross-referencing cumbersome. There are two frequently recommended junior encyclopedias:

- *Compton's Encyclopedia* (grades 5–10). Encyclopedia Britannica Educational Corporation.
- *World Book Encyclopedia* (grades 4–12). World Book.

By the time adolescents enter high school, an adult encyclopedia is an important study tool. Though the encyclopedia should never be more than the beginning place for research, it can act as an excellent supplement to textbooks in all disciplines. Throughout middle school, junior high, and the early years of high school, the junior encyclopedia may be used daily. However, an adult encyclopedia will be used with increasing frequency. Many excellent adult encyclopedias are available. The following checklist will help you select an appropriate encyclopedia for an adolescent.

A CHECKLIST FOR PURCHASING AN ENCYCLOPEDIA

- The adolescent will be able to read and understand the material in the encyclopedia.
- The material is accurate.
- Each entry presents the most essential information.
- The encyclopedia is cross-referenced in a way the adolescent can understand.
- The encyclopedia is well written and enjoyable to read.
- Pictures, maps, graphs, and charts are appropriately placed, fully identified, and easy to understand.
- Each entry makes readers want to learn more about the topic.
- The first paragraph of each entry clearly explains the important points of the entry.
- The encyclopedia meets the adolescent's educational and personal needs.
- The material is up-to-date.
- The encyclopedia can be updated with supplements.
- The encyclopedia is likely to be useful for many years.

Atlas. Good atlases include more than maps; they are helpful resources for adolescents studying geography, history, and science. *Student World Atlas* (Rand McNally, paper) and *Students Indexed World Atlas* (grades 7–12, American Map, paper) are particularly good for junior and senior high school students. *Rand McNally Classroom Atlas* is slightly less complete; it is better for students in grades five through eight. *The New York Times Atlas of the World: Family Edition* (Random House) is an atlas that can be used by the whole family. As with dictionaries and encyclopedias, adult atlases are often too complicated for adolescents. However, by the time teens reach the upper levels of high school, they need specialized information. Therefore, both a student atlas and a complete adult atlas are helpful additions to a home library.

This checklist will help you select an appropriate atlas for an adolescent.

A CHECKLIST FOR PURCHASING AN ATLAS
- Maps include all the regions of the world and are easy to read and understand.
- The atlas contains material at an appropriate maturity level for the adolescent.
- Narrative sections are located near appropriate maps and are easy to read and understand.
- The atlas has a good index.
- Cross-references are easy to locate.
- Supplemental information—such as climate, population, agricultural products, and capitals—is easy to locate and understand.
- If the atlas is an adult atlas, additional information is included (politically related areas, changes in countries due to war and politics, energy production, trade routes, air connections, surface configuration, natural vegetations).
- Illustrations are accurate and help readers understand the material.
- The material is up-to-date.

Almanacs. These inexpensive resources are filled with interesting facts about hundreds of topics. Most almanacs are updated annually and include a detailed index. The two most popular almanacs for home use are *The Information Please Almanac: The New Universe of Information* (Houghton Mifflin) and *The World Almanac and Book of Facts* (Pharos Books and St. Martin's).

Since almanacs are so easy to use, junior versions are rarely necessary. However, annual updating is. If an adolescent is reluctant to take on an adult almanac, you can purchase reasonably priced almanacs devoted to single subjects of interest, such as football. Almanacs designated specifically for young people, such as the *Facts Plus: An Almanac of Essential Information* by Susan C. Anthony (grades 3–9, Instructional Resources Company), may be enjoyed by pre- and early adolescents. An unusual almanac that almost all adolescents enjoy is the *Guinness Book of World Records*, updated annually (Bantam, paper).

Books for enjoyment. A child's first books are usually purchased by parents, grandparents, or adult friends. Most adults do not hesitate to purchase books for preschool children, but book purchases by adults tend to decrease by the time children reach late elementary school. This is unfortunate since preadolescents frequently have difficulty selecting interesting books for themselves.

Books for adolescents need not be expensive. Paperback books for young adults usually cost between $3.50 and $4.50. They cost even less when purchased through book clubs (many student book clubs are available through schools) or at used-book stores. Hardcover books for young adults rarely cost more than $15.00.

Since hardcover books will be kept for many years, parents and adolescents should be sure books purchased in hardcover are ones the teen wants added to his or her personal library. I suggest that adolescents who are building personal libraries first borrow hardcover books from the public or school library to be sure these are books they want to read again and again.

· · · · · ·
Where to Buy Books

Bookstores
There are many types of bookstores. The two most common are locally owned bookstores and bookstore chains. There are major differences in how they select and stock books.

Owners of local bookstores are concerned with the reading interests of the local population. They usually stock books from a variety of distributors and publishers. They may not have a large number of copies of a single title, but they are likely to stock a broad range of books. Some specialize in books for young people; others carry only books for adults. Most local bookstores are willing to order books that are not in stock. Local bookstores rarely discount books. However, they are likely to carry a broader range of material than do chain stores and usually offer more personalized services.

Chain bookstores are stocked through distribution centers that are concerned about the volume of book sales across the country. Since individuals rarely buy young adult hardcovers, chain bookstores do not stock them and often are unable to order them. Chain bookstores tend to have a large number of individual paperback titles by the most popular authors. If you want a recent young adult paperback, you are likely to find it in or be able to order it through a chain bookstore.

A recent phenomenon in bookstores is the discount bookstore. These bookstores purchase overstocked or out-of-print books, which they sell at reduced prices. Although you cannot count on finding a particular book or author in these bookstores, you may be able to locate some inexpensive young adult books, particularly in hardcover.

Nonbookstore Sources

Best-selling young adult books, particularly series books, are often sold in supermarkets, drugstores, and discount department stores. Books in these stores are likely to include formula books, television or movie tie-in books, and other best-selling titles.

Used-book stores are good sources for reasonably priced books. Some have a large stock of young adult paperbacks, although they aren't always shelved in separate sections. Therefore, you need to be familiar with specific titles and authors so you recognize them on the shelves.

Libraries sometimes sell books that have not been checked out recently, duplicate copies, or donated books. You may want to watch for advertisements for public library book sales in the local newspaper, on bulletin boards in your public library, or in library newsletters. Since libraries must cull books from the shelves in order to have room for new purchases, they often sell hardback young adult books for a fraction of their original purchase price.

Book fairs are another source of paperback books for adolescents. These increasingly popular events are sponsored by a school or a library that invites a distributor to display books for sale. Books here tend to be less expensive than in bookstores.

Paperback book clubs are the largest distributors of paperback books for young people in the United States. Most book clubs operate through classrooms. At regular intervals, the book club sends teachers an annotated list of books, and students receive flyers that describe the books and the authors. Students give completed order forms to the teacher, who orders for the group. Premiums are given if enough books are ordered. The two most popular book clubs for adolescents are Teen Age Book Club, Scholastic Inc. (P.O. Box 7503, Jefferson City, MO 65102) and Troll Book Clubs, Inc. (2 Lethblidge Plaza, Mahwah, New Jersey 07430).

Book clubs offer books ranging from comics to classics. Parents should supervise what adolescents order to ensure that they select a wide variety of books, not only those that are most popular with classmates.

Books from book clubs are less expensive than books in bookstores. Since book clubs typically purchase the right to publish a book from the original publisher, the quality of the binding, paper, and illustrations can be inferior to books in bookstores, but this keeps the cost down. Book clubs offer a wonderful opportunity for adolescents to develop a book-buying habit.

Some book clubs, notably the Junior Literary Guild (666 Fifth Avenue, New York, New York 10103), sell hardcover books for adolescents. Members receive books selected by book club editors, which means the books are free from controversy and should appeal to all readers. The Junior Literary Guild features books on three levels: ages 9–10, 11–12, and 12 and up. Selections include fiction and nonfiction titles of general interest. They are sent for a specified monthly charge (plus shipping) that is considerably below bookstore prices. The major advantages of belonging to a book club are reduced costs and regular book purchases. The major disadvantage is that members always receive the selected book, whether they want it or not, unless they notify the club before the book is sent. Likewise, the book club selections are limited to what the editors think the membership will purchase.

Many adolescents can also find selections of interest in adult book clubs such as the Book of the Month Club and the Literary Guild. Another popular book club of interest to adolescents is the Kids' Club, Walden Book Company (201 High Ridge Road, Samford, Connecticut 06905).

Catalogs from many mail order firms, museums, and department stores offer books. Some mail order firms that specialize in books offer discount prices for books ordered in sets. If you are a member of a book club, you probably already receive many of these catalogs. If you'd like to receive them, most mail order firms will send catalogs at no charge.

Home libraries are important. Books we have saved throughout the years are a mark of who we are and what we have become. Personal libraries mature and grow with individuals. Parents and adolescents who are aware of the variety of sources for purchasing books can begin building an excellent home library without great cost. Young adults who actively start a home library today will be "inveterate, chronic" readers tomorrow.

FOUR

Books for Teens
and Preteens

10

· ·

The Teenager's
World of Books

Young adult literature is transitional literature. By its nature, it should move the reader closer to maturity and not only by its subject matter and philosophy, but also by its inventiveness of style, its characterization, sensitivity and discovery, and most of all, by the commitment of its writers to do their best work.

Sue Ellen Bridgers

What Is Young Adult Literature?

G. Robert Carlsen says that young adult literature (also called adolescent or juvenile literature) is best defined as literature read by young adults. In other words, young adult literature includes books written specifically for adolescents as well as those for children, adults, or a general audience. While it is true that adolescents read all kinds of books, there is a body of literature with specific characteristics that make it particularly appropriate for adolescents.

Though not all young adult books are alike, they have a number of common characteristics: simple plots, characters who are young or who experience situations of the young, stories told from the viewpoint of young characters, stories that never talk down to adolescents, modern themes that relate to the lives of young readers, chapter beginnings and endings that keep readers turning pages, mature format in terms of shape of the book and spareness of pictures, easy-to-read text (short chapters, clear type, more white space), simplicity of language, eye-catching covers.

It is important to emphasize that "simple" does not mean less artistic or less literary. The best adolescent literature is as literary as the best adult literature.

What to Look for in Books for Young Adults

In general, books for young adults should have the following characteristics:

Character

PROTAGONIST
- young (usually one to two years older than the reader)
- larger than life
- realistic
- easy for reader to identify with

OTHER CHARACTERS
- usually less developed
- parents are often undeveloped, out of the picture, or single-dimensional (seen only through the eyes of the protagonist)
- other adult may serve as mentor for the adolescent
- peers may serve as friends or antagonists

Plot

- usually a single plot line
- realistic
- fast moving

- problems of interest to adolescent reader
- readers can place themselves in the plot
- lots of dialogue

Point of View
- usually the protagonist's
- often in first person
- sometimes third person, with an omniscient narrator

Voice
- usually the protagonist's
- sometimes the voice is of a more mature protagonist or second self
- often the voice is the author's
- the voice speaks directly to the reader; it is never condescending

Themes
- coming of age
- "you are not alone"
- "You can!"
- building self-esteem
- "Life is not so serious"
- "Know thyself"
- awareness
- acceptance
- developing relationships
- survival
- otherness and likeness
- heroism
- discovery—the quest

Format
- easy-to-read text, short chapters, clear type, more white space than adult books
- adult appearance

Writing Style
- Tight, simple, lively language
- Limited descriptions
- Good, honest writing by an author who cares about adolescents

. . . . . .

Books for the Stages of Adolescent Development

Books for adolescents parallel the three stages of adolescent development identified by Robert Havighurst: Preadolescence (ages 10–13), early adolescence (ages 13–15), and late adolescence (ages 15–18). Books must reflect teenagers' interests and concerns, and since adolescents' needs change rapidly, the maturity of the books they read must grow with them. As parents, we are concerned with helping our youngsters select books appropriate for their level of maturity. Chapters 11 and 12 list hundreds of books for adolescents with an appropriate age range indicated for each.

Preadolescence

Books for preadolescents often deal with the variety of problems these youngsters face. Since these books are concerned with the preadolescent's transition from childhood to young adulthood, they are often called coming-of-age books. During this period, preadolescents are torn between leaving the shelter of childhood and exploring the relationship of emerging adolescence. These are the years when a youngster may go to a school dance Friday evening and play with dolls Saturday afternoon.

Many young adult books deal with preadolescents' emerging independence and rapidly changing bodies. The best of these books help preadolescents deal with the confusion they feel. They present characters who still enjoy the games of childhood, who ask questions about their changing bodies, who are in conflict with parents and teachers, who are unsure of their friends, and who learn to deal with these problems—often with the help of caring adults. Judy Blume is well known for books dealing with preadolescence. *Are You There, God? It's Me, Margaret* is the story of a girl who is faced with her rapidly developing body, moving to a new town, making friends, and her parents' different religions. The protagonist in Blume's *Then Again, Maybe I Won't* deals with similar problems from the preteenage male perspective. (An annotated bibliography of preadolescent coming-of-age books appears in chapter 11.)

Many preadolescents' concerns and interests are like those they experienced as children. They are still interested in friendships with the same sex, slumber parties, games, animals, sports, daring adventures, camp, school, being part of the family, and having fun. Consequently, many books for this stage reflect these interests and concerns.

A large number of preadolescents read books that are parts of series. Most of these books, whether romance or adventure, fall into the category of formula fiction. In other words, the books follow a particular outline in terms of plot structure and character development. In fact, many of these books are not written by the author whose name appears on the cover. For example, many parents of today's adolescents read Nancy Drew or Hardy Boys books as older children or preadolescents. Many probably buy the updated versions of these formula books for their children today. These books were produced by the Stratemeyer Syndicate.

Unknown authors were provided with plot outlines, which they "fleshed out" to create the book. Those of us who loved these books know there is nothing detrimental about reading them. However, there is a danger if the adolescent becomes stuck on formula books such as these or most other series books. Usually adolescents outgrow these books, but often they do not know how to find more mature and literary books of interest to them. If your preadolescent is reading Nancy Drew books, examine the list of good mysteries for adolescents in chapter 11. Suggest some of these to her. If she is reading romance series books or humorous series books, suggest more literary books in these genres. If your son is reading adventure or sports series books, turn to these genres in chapter 11 for books you can suggest to him.

Early Adolescence

Early adolescence is often a lonely and frustrating time for young adults attempting to establish a personal identity as well as a place with their peers. Often adolescents feel isolated, as if no one else has ever faced the conflicts they are experiencing. Young adult books can help them feel less alone while helping them develop mature reading interests.

Many young adult problem novels deal with this difficult period in life. Characters in these books tend to be approximately the same age as and experience problems similar to those of the readers.

Authors of young adult books become anonymous mentors who are able to speak to early adolescents as no adult on the scene can. They do this by talking through their young characters, not by talking down to readers. The best young adult books are written from the perspective of a young protagonist who is on eye level with readers.

It is only in adulthood that we can reflect on our own adolescence and understand it. Author Jerry Spinelli can talk to adolescents in a way that parents, teachers, and most other adults in a young person's life cannot. He does it through the voices and actions of his young characters. Should he forget who he is as he writes and become Jerry Spinelli, father and adult author, young readers would immediately recognize the change. But this is not likely because Spinelli knows his readers and his characters too well; he remembers his own adolescence. He talks about his adolescence from his adult writer's perspective: "Like an old Brenda Lee 45, we spin on our backs for five seconds—looking back, that's all it seems, doesn't it—and then—poof!—we're grown up. But it was a glorious five seconds while it lasted—glorious and funny and excruciating and fascinating and significant. Worth remembering. Worth paying attention to. Worth writing about. Worth reading about."

In the best young adult books, the characters are worth reading about. They are young adults experiencing adolescence, and adolescence is rarely boring. Good young adult literature is honest; its characters are real people. Spinelli talks about creating such characters: "Does the writer wish to know people? Simple. Start with a single kid. Pick one out. Any one. Get to know him. All his colors and shading, all his moments. Because each kid is a population unto himself, a walking cross section, a demographic grab bag, a child's bedroom is as much a window to the universe as a scientist's lab or a philosopher's study." Spinelli's characters speak to readers through the pages of the book. At the same time, Spinelli—the third person, anonymous adult—is speaking.

When they read young adult literature, early adolescents can share their problems with other young people, the characters in the book. Characters help adolescents examine their own problems with increased objectivity, allowing them to see them from a different perspective. And, since the protagonist has the mature perspective of the author, problems are likely to be viewed broadly in relation to all life has in store. Jesse, the ten-year-old protagonist in Katherine Paterson's *Bridge to Terabithia*, reflects on the death of his best friend, Leslie:

> Now it was time for him to move out. She wasn't there, so he must go for both of them. It was up to him to pay back to the world in beauty and caring what Leslie had loaned him in vision and strength.
>
> As for the terrors ahead—for he did not fool himself that they were all behind him—well, you just have to stand up to your fear and not let it squeeze you white. Right, Leslie?

These are mature thoughts for a ten-year-old, but Jesse is not just any ten-year-old; he is a very real character in a book. Though most ten-year-olds are unlikely to think the thoughts of Jesse, the hundreds of adolescents with whom I have discussed the book believe that the words are Jesse's and that they, like Jesse, can "see beyond to the shining world—huge and terrible and beautiful and very fragile. . . ."

Late Adolescence

In late adolescence teens begin to incorporate themselves into the adult community. During this period, young adults must make decisions that affect the rest of their lives. Too often they fail to consider the possible consequences of their actions and then find themselves in situations that force them to assume adult roles. A young man and woman who have not questioned their love and sexual attraction may find themselves parents of an unwanted infant. A teenager who quits school may be unable to find a job that allows him to pay his bills.

Skilled authors are able to place late adolescent characters in situations common among teenagers and help readers discover the questions they must ask when faced with similar problems. Often the characters do not select the answers that are best for them and must suffer the consequences of their decisions, but in good adolescent literature there are always consequences.

Robert Lipsyte, a sports commentator and author of young adult books, claims that today's young people know the right answers but they don't know the right questions. He attempts to provide late adolescents with these questions.

Young adults' questions have no easy answers; often the "right" answers produce negative consequences. For example, in Robert Cormier's *The Chocolate War*, Jerry decides to oppose the powerful gang that rules his school. Readers never doubt the "rightness" of Jerry's decision. But Jerry suffers consequences; he is beaten by a member of the gang, and most of the adults in his life do not support his decision. The road of the righteous is often difficult. Cormier provides no answers, but the questions are clear to the reader.

As parents, most of us would like to shield our teenagers from situations in which they must ask these difficult questions. But in the real world people must learn to face difficult situations, ask appropriate questions, seek answers, and accept consequences. Teenagers who are unable to accomplish these tasks are not likely to become successful adults. Adolescents can share their problems with the characters in young adult books and discover that they are not alone.

· · · · · ·

Reading Young Adult Books Can Help Parents

Parents can read books written for young adults to learn to better understand their teenaged children. Every year I teach a course in adolescent literature to adults, and there are always several students who are parents of adolescents. This is what one of them wrote to me at the end of the course:

The books you asked us to read opened my eyes not only to wonderful books by wonderful writers, but to my 15-year-old son. Why didn't I remember my own adolescence? Why did it take me reading about someone else's to help me understand Rick? I don't know the answers. But, whatever they are, I am so thankful to have discovered these books. Rick and I are now reading *Killing Mr. Griffin* together. Discussing it with him is a real eye-opener. Now, if I could only convince his father to read them!

Pat Scales, a middle school librarian in South Carolina who runs a program that encourages parents to read and discuss adolescent books, suggests the following:

- Ask your teen to name his or her favorite book or a book he or she recommends you should read.
- Read the book and focus your thoughts on the adolescent main character.
- Think about your own adolescence in comparison with the main character and the experiences of your own teen.

For many of us, the doors of conversation with our adolescents have been closed. Reading and sharing adolescent books can increase understanding and open doors to meaningful discussion. Scales suggests the following to help open this door between parents and adolescents:

- Discuss the book with your teenager.
  Why was this particular book a favorite?
  How real is the main character in today's or yesterday's teenage world?
  Does the novel provide an identification with life or an escape from reality?
  What do you think the author is saying to the reader?

- Keep the discussions going by asking your teenager for reading suggestions. You may want to suggest a specific topic, or may desire to continue reading his or her special choices.

Young adult literature has the potential to guide our teenagers as they strive to meet the needs of social affection and self-esteem and to help us as we strive to understand them and what they are going through.

. . . . . .

Types of Young Adult Books

The world of young adult literature is rich. It includes all types of literature. According to author Richard Peck, the world of the adolescent is reflected in young adult books with characters who are able to deal with the world using the wisdom of the books' adult authors. Similarly, because the authors of young adult books understand that their readers' lives are just beginning, the books usually end on a positive note that prepares "both protagonist and reader for a lot of life yet to be lived. The events [in the book] are a few experiences that nudge him or thrust him toward maturity."

What makes adolescent literature special is the authors' ability to develop simple plots that become vehicles for the development of characters and their relationships. The best of these books make important points without preaching or talking down to their readers. They also create settings that transport egocentric adolescents to new worlds and allow readers to see these worlds through the eyes of realistic protagonists who possess insight and maturity beyond their years.

The Problem Novel

Think of the term *young adult literature*. What comes to mind? For many it is the problem novel—the novel that mirrors the difficult problems of adolescence. Indeed, the problem novel is the largest genre within the young adult field and during the 1970s the most predominant. No similar genre exists in adult literature. In fact, the concept of a problem novel is almost a redundancy since all novels with plots must have a problem.

Today, however, young adult problem novels are less likely to be published, and when they are they are considerably different from many of the earlier problem novels. There was a time when the plots of most young adult novels focused on a single problem. The problems addressed in the novels ranged from physical characteristics of puberty to sexuality, from pregnancy to parenthood, from rape to drugs. The list of problems examined in adolescent literature was as endless as the list of problems experienced by the adolescent. These problems are still addressed in young adult books, and new problems such as eating disorders, AIDS, and incest have been added to the list. Most of today's problem novels, and those written in the 1970s and 1980s that are still popular today, deal with these problems in honest, realistic, often humorous ways. The best of the genre attempt to help young readers see beyond their problems. They have well-rounded characters who often do not solve their problems but, instead, learn to live with them. These novels do not provide pat answers for adolescent readers nor do they guarantee happiness ever after, but they do convince readers that they are not alone.

WHAT TO LOOK FOR IN GOOD PROBLEM NOVELS

Character

PROTAGONIST
- matures as he or she deals with the problem
- experiences epiphany, often surprise at the nature of the problem
- loses innocence
- experiences catharsis, often not related to solving the problem

ANTAGONIST
- sometimes the problem itself
- person who causes the problem
- often unknown or unrecognized by protagonist

OTHER CHARACTERS
- someone who helps the protagonist deal with the problem; often a peer, an adult mentor, or a family member, although not often a parent

Plot

- problem of the protagonist is central to the plot
- individuals and relationships are affected by the problem
- problem gets worse before it gets better
- the apparent problem is often not the real problem
- ends with a resolution, though not necessarily a solution or the resolution the protagonist predicted or desired

Point of View

- usually protagonist's
- sometimes person who helps the protagonist

Voice
- often second self or more mature protagonist
- sometimes person who helps or attempts to help the protagonist

Theme
- "You are not alone"
- "Though the problem may not be solved, you can learn to deal with it"
- "You grow as a person because of trying to deal with the problem"
- "You can!"

The "Good Cry" Novel

Adolescents are very emotional, and because they are many of the books they read are also emotional. Therefore, one can group certain young adult novels into a genre that exists only in the field of young adult literature: the "good cry" novel. These novels, read particularly by girls, provide the reader with a good cry. The themes of death, broken relationships, handicaps, and young adults "making it" despite the odds against them appeal to the sentimentality of the young adult reader. As young adult author Richard Peck says, "To oversimplify, after a reassuring outcome in a story, I suspect . . . [the young adults] like best a good cry." These novels have characteristics similar to the problem novel, but tend to have more emotional appeal.

WHAT TO LOOK FOR IN GOOD "GOOD CRY" NOVELS

Character

PROTAGONIST
- realistic
- vulnerable, but also strong

- at the mercy of circumstance
- possesses a humorous side
- normal and usually happy
- loses innocence

ANTAGONIST
- often not a recognizable person; maybe society, disease, unforeseen death, the law, and so on
- not always recognized by the protagonist

OTHER CHARACTERS
- often a mentor adult
- often a close friend

Plot
- provides the background or point of reference for the character and reader
- emphasizes emotions of character
- development of protagonist is central

Point of View
- the protagonist's
- that of close friend or peer

Voice
- older, more experienced protagonist or second self
- close friend or peer

Theme
- metamorphosis
- maturation
- epiphany
- "In spite of trials you can survive"

Humor

Adolescence can be looked at as a period of change and struggle. However, it is also filled with humor. Humorous fiction allows adolescents to deal with the problems of their lives from a different perspective. However, understanding the humor of adolescence can be difficult for writers of young adult realistic fiction. As Jerry Spinelli, author of humorous books for young adults, writes, if adults attempt to determine why an adolescent takes the last drop of root beer from the bottle but leaves the bottle in the refrigerator, for example, "speculation may be exercising but is invariably fruitless, for this is the twilight zone where the adult, with all his superior powers of insight, begins to lose contact with the juvenile psyche." This is also the humor of the adolescent. It is the task of the author of humorous fiction to enter the psyche of the adolescent in order to tell about events from the adolescent's perspective. For adults who read the books of authors like Jerry Spinelli, we, too, can better understand and laugh at elements of the adolescent's behavior we often find irksome. By helping young readers see the humorous side of adolescence, writers, through their characters, can take readers outside of themselves so that they, along with the characters, can mature beyond adolescence. Parents can help adolescents find humorous novels that will not only allow them to laugh at themselves, but will help them mature toward adulthood.

WHAT TO LOOK FOR IN GOOD HUMOROUS FICTION

Character

PROTAGONIST
- young
- identifiable
- caught up in real situations

- realistic
- does things reader does or would like to do

OTHER CHARACTERS

- adults are often undeveloped; when developed, are portrayed as real people
- often an adult other than a parent acts as a mentor
- one or more characters act as foils to the protagonist

Plot

- situational
- wide-ranging
- humor found in situations that are not innately humorous
- novel may not be written to be humorous; however, sense of humor helps the character mature
- often an element of suspense

Point of View

- protagonist's

Voice

- protagonist's

Theme

- "You can survive"
- "Life is not so serious"
- "There are other kids who share your problems"

Coming-of-Age

Many young adult books deal with the developing adolescent and problems caused by the transition from childhood to adulthood. Characters in coming-of-age books usually progress through a series of events to reach more mature understanding. Literature can help egocentric adolescents see beyond the moment and understand the consequences of their actions. At the same time, these books can make adolescent readers feel less alone.

WHAT TO LOOK FOR IN GOOD COMING-OF-AGE NOVELS

Character

PROTAGONIST
- maturing from one phase of development to the next
- confused
- often unsure about physical changes
- is developing sexuality
- exhibits psychological growth and changing emotions and values
- rebellious
- seeking yet fearful of independence
- afraid but puts up a good front
- loses innocence but gains experience

ANTAGONIST
- often the situation in which the adolescent finds himself rather than a character
- often the perceived antagonist is not the real antagonist
- adult (parent, teacher, or other)
- former friend
- self
- society or culture (family, school, community)

OTHER CHARACTERS
- individual who allows growth to occur
- often initially assumed to be the antagonist
- mentor adult
- best friend

Plot
- situations that impede development
- situations that encourage development (often unrecognized by protagonist)
- separation from society (through peer group association, a journey, et cetera)

- some things remain the same while others change dramatically
- initiation may be social, religious, political
- reversal common
- values change
- protagonist may choose to remain outside of society

Setting
- more important than in other young adult novels
- often physically and symbolically isolated from society (on an island, boat, et cetera)
- often associated with peer group (at school, camp, hangout, et cetera)

Point of View
- protagonist's
- sometimes alternate points of view interspersed with protagonist's

Voice
- protagonist's
- second self
- omniscient

Theme
- often not explicitly stated
- developing a values system
- self-knowledge
- deeper meaning of life

Style and Language
- protagonist often takes a real or symbolic journey
- humor interspersed
- language reflects theme
- characters speak in vernacular

Historical Fiction

Though historical novels for young adults have been published for many years, they are gaining new popularity. This may be because the authors are increasingly aware of the needs and interests of their young readers. An increasing number of writers of young adult historical fiction are concerned with the historic accuracy of the work. Authors Christopher Collier and James Lincoln Collier provide a good example of recent trends in historical fiction for young adults. Their protagonists are young; they appear in accurate historic settings and face problems they would have faced in those settings, but they deal with these problems in ways today's young adults can understand. Historic fiction can bring history to life for adolescents while it helps them deal more objectively with their own problems.

WHAT TO LOOK FOR IN GOOD HISTORICAL FICTION

Purpose
- bring history to life
- change reader's opinions

Character

PROTAGONIST
- fictional
- realistic adolescent who could have lived during the period
- heroic; larger than life
- has concerns and problems of typical adolescent
- accessible to the reader

OTHER CHARACTERS
- major characters are usually fictional
- minor characters may be real figures from history

Plot
- fictional character is placed in real historic situation (war, political conflict, social unrest, et cetera)
- sequence of events in which character is involved is historically possible
- sequence of events occurring in the novel is plausible
- actions of any real persons are accurate and plausible
- events may be romanticized to some extent

Point of View
- usually protagonist's
- sometimes multiple points of view are presented
- third-person point of view may be needed to relate historical narrative

Voice
- often protagonist's second self viewing the event in a reflective manner
- sometimes the author or omniscient narrator

Setting
- in the past
- historically accurate (e.g., Could the character really get from point A to point B in one day?)

Theme
- patriotism, regionalism, heroism
- "War is evil"
- "You can!"

Multicultural

Adolescents prefer books with characters who are more like they are. They want the characters and the situations in these books to mirror their lives not necessarily as they are but as they would like them to be. The egocentrism of adolescence makes introducing young adults to cultures and ideas different from their own very difficult. However, if adolescents do not learn about cultural differences, they are likely to have difficulty living successfully in an increasingly culturally diverse society. As Mop, one of the characters in Walter Dean Myers's *Mop, Moondance, and the Nagasaki Knights*, says to one of the baseball players on her team about playing teams from France, Japan, and Mexico, "Intercultural means that you figure out how somebody's different and let them know that you know it and don't mind too much" (p. 89).

Another reason it is essential for adolescents to be introduced to books depicting young people in a variety of cultures is so all readers can read about people within their own cultures. For generations, students in U.S. schools have read books populated by white, Eurocentric protagonists. Young readers must be able to identify with the characters and situations in the books they read. Is it any wonder that African American, Native American, and Hispanic students score lower on standardized reading tests than white students when all students have been required to read books with white protagonists and study Eurocentric history? (NAEP reading test results from 1971 through 1990 indicate that blacks and Hispanics score significantly lower than whites.) If young readers are not introduced to books with which they can identify, they are unlikely to progress beyond the egocentric stage of reading development, and they are unlikely to become mature readers.

WHAT TO LOOK FOR IN GOOD MULTICULTURAL BOOKS

Purpose
  • developing awareness
  • developing self-esteem
  • coming to terms with differences between cultures

Character

PROTAGONIST
- adolescent
- realistic
- a part of the culture in which he or she lives
- often more mature than age of character indicates
- develops self-esteem as a member of his or her culture
- may struggle with his or her differences, but learns to rejoice in them
- growth within the culture

ANTAGONIST
- usually from the majority culture
- sometimes the system or government

OTHER CHARACTERS
- peers within the culture, frequently undeveloped
- an adult mentor within the culture, usually not a parent

Plot
- often more complex than typical young adult novel
- frequently deals with confrontation between cultures (protagonist vs. antagonist; protagonist vs. reader)
- the character learns about him- or herself within the culture
- increased awareness of the culture

Point of View
- protagonist's
- often written in first person

Voice
- protagonist's
- sometimes second self, or more mature protagonist
- sometimes the mentor's voice is evident
- never preachy or dogmatic

Setting
- accurately portrays culture
- often presents clashing cultures (minority culture vs. majority culture; parents' culture vs. adolescent's culture)

Theme
- heroism
- combating prejudice and discrimination
- individual against society
- "You can!"

Mystery

Most readers of mystery read the books for escape. We read them to find out how ordinary characters placed in extraordinary situations come up with even more extraordinary solutions to problems. Probably because mysteries provide escape at the same time as they introduce us to protagonists not unlike ourselves, the genre has long been popular with young adult readers.

Mysteries are exciting, but they are also predictable. Many mystery writers write series of books with the same detective. Mysteries also follow formulaic plot lines. Therefore, the mystery genre is perfect for young readers. Readers of mysteries quickly learn that all clues are significant, even if they do not seem so at the time. If the writer has one of the characters lose her car keys prior to the murder, the loss of the keys is not included in the novel by accident. However, readers of mysteries soon figure out that some clues are planted to confuse them. Such clues even have a name: red herrings. Therefore, when a reader becomes familiar with the conventions of the mystery, reading mysteries is an easy task. It is immaterial to enjoyment of the mystery whether or not the reader can figure out the puzzle prior to the end of the novel. What is essential is that the reader become caught in the web the mystery writer is weaving.

WHAT TO LOOK FOR IN GOOD MYSTERIES

Character

PROTAGONIST
- detective; usually falls into the roll by chance
- adolescent

VICTIM(S)
- usually undeveloped
- may not even be known to the reader

SUSPECTS
- numerous suspects
- most will have nothing to do with the crime
- many are well-developed in order to mislead the protagonist or detective
- minor suspects are usually undeveloped and often in the
  background; they are rarely the murderer or perpetrator

ANTAGONIST
- murderer or perpetrator
- present throughout the book
- may be one of the better developed characters in the book
- not recognized as murderer or perpetrator until late in the
  book

Plot
- murder or mysterious event occurs early in the novel
- any character, with the exception of the detective, could
  be potential murderer or perpetrator
- every piece of information could be important in solving
  the mystery
- pieces of puzzle presented throughout the novel
- red herrings (misleading clues)
- verisimilitude; all events could be possible
- suspension of disbelief required

Point of View
- protagonist's/detective's; usually withholds information from the reader

Voice
- protagonist's/detective's

Setting
- contributes to the plot; may be an isolated island or a mysterious house
- weather is often important
- various; detective usually moves about

Theme
- usually unimportant

Suspense

Suspense novels for young adults have gained popularity in recent years. Many such stories written for adults are also popular with adolescents, but the length and complexity of plot line often makes them difficult for the immature reader. Therefore, many young adult authors have used their skills to compose suspense stories for young readers.

Although there are many similarities between suspense stories and mysteries, there are also many differences. Suspense, like mystery, catches the reader unaware. Readers of suspense must suspend disbelief in order to be caught up in the spine-tingling effect of the plot. As with mystery, suspense stories deal with the unknown. However, how the unknown is dealt with differs significantly.

Unlike in the mystery where the victim is usually undeveloped, the protagonist of the suspense story is typically the victim or the intended victim. The antagonist is usually evil and intelligent—the crime has yet to be committed. Protagonists may or may not suspect the villain. At times, the victim will not know who the antagonist is but the reader will. Characters in the suspense story are often more fully developed than in mystery. Suspense differs from most other fiction in that the antagonist may be more completely developed than the protagonist. Typically in the suspense story we anticipate the enactment of the evil deed rather than attempt to determine who committed the crime. The plot of the suspense story is often more complex than the plot of the mystery. Literary techniques such as foreshadowing and flashback are often employed.

WHAT TO LOOK FOR IN GOOD SUSPENSE

Character

PROTAGONIST
- victim (readers may not know he or she is a victim until late in the novel)
- adolescent
- vulnerable; isolated
- evokes reader empathy

ANTAGONIST
- bold
- insensitive
- exceptionally cunning, insightful, manipulative
- believable
- well developed
- peer of protagonist and reader
- often someone the protagonist and reader cares about

Plot
- several subplots common
- foreshadowing and flashbacks used
- buildup of tension and uncertainty

- clues given (may be misleading)
- character development important to plot
- chapters begin with hooks and end with cliff-hangers
- setting is important
- title is often a clue

Point of View
- protagonist's/victim's
- sometimes omniscience is also employed (reader knows what victim does not)

Voice
- protagonist's/victim's

Setting
- important to the plot
- creates sense of foreboding

Theme
- often unimportant
- sometimes subplot provides the theme
- "Things and people are not always what they seem"

Romance

Teenage romances are vastly popular with adolescent female readers. Critics of these books suggest several reasons why romances are so popular.

- Young adults are seeking escapism. Just as young male readers select adventures for escape reading, young female readers select romance to escape from the unpleasant realities of their day-to-day lives.
- The success of adult romance series may be another reason for the success of young adult romances. In fact, several publish-

ers market adult romances and young adult romances together in bookstores. One publisher commented that mothers who read adult romances tend to recommend teen romances to their daughters.

• Romances appeal to young women because they usually depict desirable relationships without the complication of sexual involvement.

• Romances provide simple reading for adolescents. They are predictable and contain a "code" of romance, sexuality, and beautification: the woman gets her man if she behaves in certain predictable ways. In the more literary romances, however, girls are brighter, stronger, and career-oriented.

Parents can help adolescents find more mature romances that have some of the predictable characteristics of series romances but are more literary with more mature themes. Good young adult romances do not follow a specific formula, although they do contain many of the characteristics young readers seek in romance novels. Good young adult romances provide the kind of escape from day-to-day life that good suspense books provide; they have ordinary characters in often extraordinary situations.

WHAT TO LOOK FOR IN GOOD YOUNG ADULT ROMANCE

Characters

PROTAGONIST
• female adolescent
• realistic; flawed
• appearance is inconsequential
• intelligent; interested in education and career
• faces important problems in and outside of the romance
• sometimes reason and emotion conflict
• not stereotyped; multidimensional

ROMANTIC INTEREST
- teenage male
- realistic; flawed
- appearance is inconsequential
- may or may not provide a positive relationship for young woman (if positive, values her strength; if negative, may be physically and psychologically damaging)
- not stereotyped; multidimensional

FAMILY
- varied social and economic backgrounds
- realistic
- relationships between family members is often strained
- family relationships may provide a subplot
- not stereotyped; multidimensional

Plot
- more than one plot line
- main plot often centers on a moral dilemma
- love relationship is often difficult
- love relationship is realistic; sexual relationship is neither avoided nor exploited

Point of View
- protagonist's
- third person

Voice
- protagonist's
- sometimes older, wiser self

Literary Elements
- figurative language
- motifs (hazy light, seasons, darkness, et cetera)

Theme
- varied
- "There is more to life than romantic love"
- "Individuals must develop outside of relationships"

Fantasy

There was a time when fantasy was considered inappropriate for any other than young children. This is no longer the case. When Madeleine L'Engle wrote *A Wrinkle in Time* in the 1960s, fantasy was established as an acceptable genre for young adult readers. Fantasy is far more than escape literature. It is literature that instructs through the use of allegory, or extended metaphor. Although the fantasy usually begins in the real world, the characters are transported to another world, created by the author, in a magical moment. The other world of the fantasy is a world unlike the real world, but a world in which the problems of the hero are metaphors for the problems of the readers.

Like all young adult books, fantasies have young characters who deal with the problems of young readers. Since the major literary technique of the fantasy plot is a quest for good and for truth, there is probably no genre more appropriate to meet the needs of adolescents. What is adolescence if it is not a quest to discover who you are and where you fit into the world? Through fantasy literature, adolescents can find unexpected answers to their quest.

WHAT TO LOOK FOR IN GOOD FANTASY

Characters

PROTAGONIST
- represents every adolescent ("everyman")
- usually a reluctant, self-doubting hero or heroine

- possesses characteristics of good and evil
- transforms self by encountering and defeating problems
- although humanlike, may possess superhuman characteristics (some of which are discovered during the course of the adventure)
- very well developed

ANTAGONIST
- may or may not be human
- may not be recognized by the protagonist until late in the novel

OTHERS
- usually part of either the real world or other world, but rarely both

Plot
- begins in the waking world
- a magical moment occurs when the protagonist transcends the real world and enters the other world
- most suspense develops in other world
- involves quest to solve problems and conquer evil
- life-and-death situations are encountered
- events have many levels of meaning
- protagonist's growth is central to the plot
- protagonist may not conquer evil by the end of novel
- conclusion may be a resting place for the beginning of new quests in subsequent novels

Point of View
- protagonist's

Voice
- author's

Setting
- both real and other worlds are believable
- moment of transcendence from real to other world must appear to be possible
- wide-ranging
- magical world must follow rules set by author
- there may be talking animals, magical or mythological beasts

Literary Elements
- allegory (imaginary world makes the real world more visible or understandable)
- invented words or a new language may be used
- language is often central to the plot and theme

Theme
- relates to hero's quest
- involves self-transformation and self-awareness
- "Problems in the real world can be conquered"
- "Good can triumph over evil"

Science Fiction

Science fiction is literature of the imagination. Writers of science fiction make connections between the world as we know it and the world they create. According to young adult science fiction writer William Sleator, "Science fiction is literature about something that hasn't happened yet, but might be possible some day. That it might be possible is the important part." Science fiction is based in scientific knowledge—what we know about our universe. It could happen.

Science fiction, like fantasy, allows readers to leave their limited universe and enter a world of limitless possibilities. The char-

acters are realistic, but the obstacles they surmount are beyond
the scope of the adolescent. The solutions they pursue often help
real teenagers deal with everyday problems. Science fiction differs
from fantasy in that the world is described according to the natural laws of science. Usually the world is in an advanced scientific
state; the fantastic things that happen are possible given what we
know about science. Adolescents who are interested in science
are often avid readers of science fiction. Likewise, readers of science fiction often develop an interest in the science on which
the fiction is based.

CHARACTERISTICS OF GOOD SCIENCE FICTION
FOR YOUNG ADULTS

Characters

PROTAGONIST
- adolescent
- believable, similar to the reader
- has superhuman qualities that are humanly possible (e.g.:
  extreme intelligence, bravery, psychic abilities, insight)
- may be the victim
- has real human problems

ANTAGONIST
- not always a person, sometimes a situation or the setting
- that which must be overcome by the protagonist
- evil
- alien
- may be other self of the protagonist

Plot
- based on the laws of science
- events are plausible
- requires suspension of disbelief

- begins in the real world as the reader knows it
- follows rules set by the author, which must have a foundation in the laws of science
- fast-moving, exciting

Point of View
- protagonist's
- third person
- omniscient

Voice
- protagonist's
- sometimes second, older, or wiser self

Setting
- based on the laws of science
- moves from reader's real world to imaginary world
- often set in past or future

Theme
- "Science has important effects on our lives"
- "We can better understand our world by examining other imaginary but possible worlds"
- "The world of the future is an outgrowth of our world today"

Nonfiction

Nonfiction is an important part of the literature written for young adults. It shares many of the characteristics and attributes of young adult fiction. High-quality nonfiction for adolescents has been available for only about twenty years. Prior to that time there was some nonfiction for children, but adolescents were expected to read material written for adults. According to W. G. Ellis, many adolescents today borrow nonfiction books more frequently than fiction from libraries.

Authors and publishers recognize the popularity of nonfiction on many topics. They also are aware that most adolescents are not yet ready for highly sophisticated adult works in the social sciences, arts, humanities, and sciences. The problems addressed in adult nonfiction are not the problems of most adolescents. Adolescents need their own nonfiction books that are stimulating and challenging and that address problems and issues from their perspectives.

The best nonfiction for adolescents is written by authorities in the fields in which they write. Many writers are known for both their adult writings and their young adult books. Most recognize the importance of introducing teenagers to issues, questions, ideas, concepts, and skills in terms they can understand. Good young adult nonfiction differs from adult nonfiction in terms of complexity, not in terms of quality of content or writing. Young adult nonfiction is not condensed from adult books. On the few occasions when adult nonfiction has been reissued for adolescents, it has been rewritten by knowledgeable writers, not simply condensed. (Many fine works of nonfiction for young adults are discussed in chapter 12.)

CHARACTERISTICS OF GOOD NONFICTION FOR YOUNG ADULTS

Readability
- appropriate for reading level of adolescents
- appropriate for developmental level of adolescents
- jargon and technical language is minimal or carefully defined
- should be of interest to individual student (does not necessarily have to interest the teacher)

High-Quality Writing
- appropriate and acceptable variety of English
- use of language adroit or distinctive

Material Logically Organized
- format allows easy access to information
- index, table of contents, and other devices help locate information
- book covers what it purports to cover

Visuals Aid in Understanding
- visuals appear with appropriate textual material
- photographs are of high reproduction quality
- visuals are clear and generally attractive
- content of visuals is easily understood

Accurate Information
- author's credentials are appropriate
- information is up-to-date for field covered
- information does not contain errors
- supporting evidence included for all assertions

Poetry

Poetry collections for young adults are a rather recent phenomenon. For many years there were few anthologies of poems appropriate for adolescents. The poems adolescents read generally appeared in school literature anthologies and were written by adult authors for adult readers. Today, a variety of poetry books are published for adolescents.

Probably the most popular type of poetry book for teens is the anthology of poems on a single theme or topic. Often these anthologies include works written by adults for adults, but these poems are selected with the interests and needs of adolescents in mind.

Similarly, anthologists have begun collecting the works of a single poet and editing them so they are appropriate for adolescents. This has made the poetry of Carl Sandburg, Emily Dickinson, Sylvia Plath, and many others accessible and interesting to young adults.

Collections of poems written specifically for adolescents are also available. Shel Silverstein is the acknowledged master of this craft for preadolescent readers. Poets such as Nancy Willard, Gary Soto, Lillian Morrison, Mel Glenn, Paul Janeczko, and Richard Peck have gained recognition for their young adult work.

In addition, anthologists have been collecting work written by young adult poets. This work has been published in anthologies dealing with specific themes or issues. (Many anthologies and poetry collections are listed in chapter 12.)

Young adult books are written for all the developmental stages of the adolescent, and every type of literature present in the adult marketplace is available to adolescent readers. The best of these books speak to adolescents from the perspective of adolescent characters, but deal with the problems of adolescence with greater maturity than most adolescents possess.

Parents who are aware of the books of young adulthood often can provide the right book at the right time. Likewise, parents who read these books are likely to gain new perspectives on their teenagers' problems and concerns, particularly when they discuss the books with their teens.

11

. . . .

Fiction Kids Love

Several thousand books for young adults are published each year, making the selection of appropriate books for preadolescent and adolescent readers challenging.

. . . . . .

How to Use This Annotated Book List

The following annotated bibliography lists good books appropriate for readers from ages ten through eighteen. It is divided into two sections: fiction (chapter 11) and nonfiction (chapter 12).

The books are further divided into genres to help you select books based on your adolescent's interests. To read more about each genre, turn to chapter 10, where descriptions of most of the genres and lists of criteria for selecting good books are included. All of the books recommended here meet the criteria of good books as outlined in chapter 10. However, not all books are appropriate for all readers.

The age, maturity, reading ability, interest, and gender of your adolescent child may influence the books you and she or he select. An indication of the general age range for which the book is appropriate is provided in each entry. This age range should guide you in selecting or suggesting books.

PA   Preadolescent (ages 10–13)
EA   Early Adolescent (ages 13–15)
LA   Late Adolescent (ages 15–18)

The year of first publication is listed after the title and author. If the book is available in paperback, the word "paper" appears after the date. Other information includes whether males (M) or females (F) are more likely to enjoy the book, a star (*) if the book is appropriate for poor readers, and a plus (+) if the book is especially good for reading aloud. A few excellent books were no longer in print when this bibliography was prepared. However, because these books are available in many libraries, the symbol (L), meaning available in libraries only, appears following the annotation.

If you want to find additional books within a genre of interest to your adolescent, go back to the appropriate good-book criteria in chapter 10. Take the list of criteria to the public library and ask the young adult librarian to suggest books that meet the criteria. Or browse through the library or a bookstore looking for other books by authors suggested in this bibliography; most writers write within a single genre, though several cross genres. Often by reading the summary on the dust jacket of a hardback or on the back cover or inside page of a paperback, you can determine whether the book might be appropriate for your adolescent. Sometimes book covers also contain positive reviews of the book. Look for terms such as "starred review" that indicate that the book was considered to be particularly good not only by the reviewer but by the review source. Also look for indication of awards won either by this book or by the author. A seal on a book is an indication that it was a Newbery Medal winner, the most prestigious literary award given to young adult books.

• • • • • •

Problem Novels

Personal Problems

The Ape Inside Me, Kin Platt. 1979. Paper.
Ed is often violent. The book is particularly good for poor readers as its vocabulary is simple, while its message is mature.   EA LA M *

Forever, Judy Blume. 1975. Paper.
Blume explores how young love leads to sexual activity.   EA LA F *

I Was a Fifteen-Year-Old Blimp, Patti Stren. 1985. Paper.
A girl is so desperate for a thinner figure and male attention that she begins a dangerous program of rapid weight loss.   PA EA F * +

If I Asked, Would You Stay?, Eve Bunting. 1984. Paper.
Though running away and suicide are prominent in this book, it is really about what trust can mean to a relationship.   LA

The Kissimmee Kid, Vera Cleaver and Bill Cleaver. 1981. Paper.
Evie must decide whether to tell the truth about her brother-in-law's cattle rustling.   PA

One Fat Summer, Robert Lipsyte. 1977. Paper.
Robert is overweight but conquers his problem when he gets a job mowing lawns. *Summer Rules* (1981; paper) is the sequel.   EA M * +

Out of Control, Norma Fox Mazer. 1993.
Valerie is assaulted by three males in her high school at the start of this powerful novel, which explores the fear, grief, guilt, and anger that occur following such an attack.   EA LA F *

The Pig-Out Blues, Jan Greenberg. 1982. Paper.

Jodie overeats when she feels disappointed. Helpful friends get her on the right track.   PA EA F *

Silver, Norma Fox Mazer. 1988. Paper.

Sarabeth must deal with being different. All the students in her school are snobby and rich and ask her questions like "Do you have a regular bathroom in your trailer?"   PA EA F

Working on It, Joan Oppenheimer. 1980. Paper.

Tracy hopes her shyness will vanish, but it does not. She takes command of her problem by signing up for drama class.   EA LA

Difficult Personal Accomplishments

MUSIC

I Will Call It Georgie's Blues, Suzanne Newton. 1983. Paper.

Though the backdrop of this book is the jazz piano Neal plays to escape his family's problems, the book is really about family relationships and the problems caused by parents who expect perfection from their children.   EA

Rock 'n' Roll Nights, Todd Strasser. 1982. Paper.

This book and its sequel, *Turn It Up!* (1984; paper), are about a talented teenage musician who is trying to make it in the competitive world of rock 'n' roll.   EA

SPORTS

Backfield Package, Thomas J. Dygard. 1992.

This well-known writer of sports books for adolescents has written a novel about teenage problems on and off the playing field. The team's star quarterback has made a pact with his teammates to go to a small college where they can continue to play together, but he is recruited by a large university. EA M

The Contender, Robert Lipsyte. 1967. Paper.

A young African American boxer learns that being a contender is more important than being a champion. Lipsyte has retold the tale in *The Brave* (1991), a more contemporary sports novel about a Native American boxer who can't control the monster within himself. EA LA * +

Halfback Tough, Thomas J. Dygard. 1986. Paper.

Football helps Joe change from a student who always violates the rules and looks down on others to one who is respected by peers and adults. EA M

Hoops, Walter Dean Myers. 1981. Paper.

Lonnie and his Harlem teammates learn about playing basketball (winning and losing) and about living from a former professional basketball player. Readers who enjoy this should also like *Scorpions* (1990). PA EA LA M *

In Lane Three, Alex Archer, Tessa Duder. 1989. Paper.

Through her female character this New Zealand author explores the competition, sacrifice, and parental pressure experienced in attempting to become an Olympic swimmer. Look for other books with the same character name in the title. PA EA

The Throwing Season, Michael French. 1980.

Indian is an outstanding shot putter. When asked to throw a competition, he refuses and is severely beaten, but he fights back to win again. EA

Tournament Upstart, Thomas Dygard. 1984. Paper.

A team from a small high school enters a major basketball tournament. EA M

Zanboomer, R. R. Knudson. 1978.

Zan is the star of a baseball team. Other books about Zan

include *Zanballer* (1986), *Zanbanger* (1977), and *Zan Hagen's Marathon* (1984).   PA EA F * L

Peer Relationships

All Together Now, Sue Ellen Bridgers. 1979. Paper.

A young tomboy befriends a mentally retarded man.   PA EA * +

The Chocolate War, Robert Cormier. 1974. Paper.

This may be the most terrifying and thought-provoking book ever written for young adults. Jerry stands up against a gang only to find that he must stand alone. The sequel, *Beyond the Chocolate War* (1985; paper), allows Jerry to resolve some of his bitterness.   LA

Father Figure, Richard Peck. 1978. Paper.

Jim finds his role as surrogate father to his eight-year-old brother is threatened when they are forced to move in with their real father.   PA EA

Hey, Dollface, Deborah Hautzig. 1978.

This novel explores the topic of lesbianism as two girls become concerned that their relationship is more than friendship.   EA LA F

Homecoming, Cynthia Voigt. 1981. Paper.

A thirteen-year-old travels many miles with her brothers and sister searching for a home. The sequel, *Dicey's Song* (1982; paper +), won the Newbery Medal for its portrayal of the life of children on Maryland's Eastern Shore.   PA EA F +

I Never Loved Your Mind, Paul Zindel. Harper & Row, 1970. Bantam, paper.

This book contains Zindel's typical cast of madcap characters, in this case two high school dropouts seeking one another.   EA

If I Love You, Am I Trapped Forever?, M. E. Kerr. 1973. Paper.

An egocentric teenager learns about himself when he trades places with a boy he dislikes.   PA EA M *

Keeping Christina, Sue Ellen Bridgers. 1993.

A story of relationships, friendship, jealousy, and suspicion makes the plot strong enough to involve adolescents. EA LA F

Long Time Between Kisses, Sandra Scoppettone. 1982.

A typical teenage girl confuses her feelings of self-negation and rebelliousness with love for a man with multiple sclerosis. EA L

Lord of the Flies, William Golding. 1954. Paper.

English schoolboys marooned on an island attempt to set up their own society. The ending is horrifyingly realistic. EA LA

No Kidding, Bruce Brooks. 1989. Paper.

Set in the middle of the twenty-first century, this novel is the story of fourteen-year-old Sam, who has his alcoholic mother institutionalized and learns how much she truly cares for him and his alcoholic-hating, religious fanatic brother. EA LA

The Outsiders, S. E. Hinton. 1967. Paper.

In this book about teenage gangs, the characters learn about the importance of life. Hinton's other books have similar plots: *That Was Then, This Is Now* (1971; paper), *Rumble Fish* (Delacorte, 1975; Dell, paper), and *Tex* (1979; paper). EA * +

Remembering the Good Times, Richard Peck. 1985. Paper.

This book traces the relationship of three close friends. No one recognizes the inner turmoil of one of them until it is too late. EA LA

Other Adults

After the Rain, Norma Fox Mazer. 1987. Paper.

In this Newbery honorable-mention book, Mazer explores the topic of losing a beloved grandparent. PA EA

Far from Home, Ouida Sebestyen. 1980. Paper.

After his mother dies, Salty sets out to find the father he has never known, only to find the unexpected love of his elderly grandmother. EA

Figure of Speech, Norma Fox Mazer. 1973. Paper.

This novel tells of a child's love for her grandfather and how she protects him when other family members attempt to push him aside. PA * + L

The Great Gilly Hopkins, Katherine Paterson. 1978. Paper.

Gilly is a foster child who has been thrown out of every foster home. Trotter, her foster mother, vows to become family to her and succeeds in helping Gilly find herself. PA EA *

LeRoy & the Old Man, W. E. Butterworth. 1980. Paper.

After witnessing a mugging, LeRoy flees to Mississippi to live with his grandfather. When the victim dies, LeRoy must decide if he will return to Chicago to testify in court. EA LA

The Man without a Face, Isabelle Holland. 1972. Paper.

Chuck feels rejected by his family and inferior to his sister. The "man without a face" tutors him for entrance exams for a prep school. They are attracted to one another and have a brief, sensitive, homosexual encounter. The book does not end with the encounter, but with Chuck's developing understanding of the meaning of love and affection. EA LA *

The Pigman, Paul Zindel. 1968. Paper.

Lorraine and John become friends with the elderly Mr. Pignati. When Mr. Pignati dies of a heart attack after they have a wild party in his home while he is away, the teenagers must deal with their guilt. In *The Pigman's Legacy* (1980; paper), John and Lorraine befriend another old man who is hiding in the Pigman's house. EA LA

Return to Bitter Creek, Doris Buchanan Smith. 1986. Paper.

Lacey is the daughter of an unmarried woman who lives with an artist. The three return to a North Carolina town to try to develop a relationship with Lacey's grandparents. EA

A Shadow like a Leopard, Myron Levoy. 1981. Paper.

Ramon is a street punk and a gifted poet who forms a relationship with an elderly artist. L. Another interesting book about relationships is *Kelly 'n' Me* (1992).　EA LA

The Son of Someone Famous, M. E. Kerr. 1974. Paper.

For Adam, being the son of someone famous is not easy. He lives with his lonely, embittered grandfather. They both grow up emotionally and develop a sense of worth.　PA EA *

What about Grandma?, Hadley Irwin. 1982. Paper.

When Grandmother refuses to live in a nursing home, Rhys and her mother spend the summer with her. It is a time of conflict and discovery for Rhys.　PA EA F *

Parents

Back Home, Michelle Magorian. 1984. Paper.

Rusty is sent to the United States from England in 1940. When she returns home after World War II, the British find her rude and abrasive. No one wants to hear about the loving family she grew up with.　EA

Dinky Hocker Shoots Smack!, M. E. Kerr. 1972. Paper.

This book is about overweight Dinky and her professional mother who is more concerned about her work than her daughter. The book's title is Dinky's cry for help.　PA EA

IOUs, Ouida Sebestyen. 1982. Paper.

Stowe is torn between his love for his mother and his desire to experiment with life.　EA

Nice Girl from Good Home, Fran Arrick. 1984. Paper.

This book describes how family members react differently to the loss of the father's job and income.　EA *

Of Love and Death and Other Journeys, Isabelle Holland. 1975.

After her mother's sudden death, Meg is sent to live with the father she has never known.　EA F L

Ordinary People, Judith Guest. 1976. Paper.

Conrad must deal with his parents' reactions to his attempted suicide. LA

Rabble Starkey, Lois Lowry. 1987. Paper.

Twelve-year-old Rabble lives with her mother, Sweet Hosanna, and the Bigelow family for whom she works. Sweet Hosanna holds both families together. Rabble comes to learn how even though her mother was only fourteen and unmarried when Rabble was born, she is a very special person. PA EA F

RoboDad, Alden R. Carter. 1990.

Carter examines an exceedingly difficult father-daughter relationship. Shar's father becomes an emotional vegetable when an artery bursts in his brain. Shar is determined to help her father become a loving dad once again. His violent outbursts after hours of hypnotic television viewing raise horrifying fears for Shar and the rest of the family. EA LA F

Sweetly Sings the Donkey, Vera Cleaver. 1985. Paper.

The Snow family inherits property in Florida and attempts to build a home on its bare acreage. PA EA

Unfinished Portrait of Jessica, Richard Peck. 1991. Paper.

Jessica blames her mother for the divorce of her parents until she is sent by her mother to Mexico to visit with the father she thinks is "perfect." She soon learns he is manipulative and immature and returns home to rebuild her relationship with her mother. EA F

Weekend Sisters, Hila Colman. 1985. Paper.

On weekends Amanda must share her father with her new step-family. She decides to leave home and let the new family sort out its problems. EA F

Social Issues

Abby, My Love, Hadley Irwin. 1985. Paper.

In this sensitive story about incest, Abby's friend Chip doesn't understand her emotional ups and downs. Also try two other

Irwin novels on difficult social issues: *Can't Hear You Listening* is about drugs (1990) and *So Long at the Fair* is about suicide (1988). EA LA *

Angel Dust Blues, Todd Strasser. 1979. Paper.

Alex is arrested for selling drugs to an undercover agent. The book, told in flashbacks, reveals how a normal high school student covers up his loneliness. EA LA M *

Bad Apple, Larry Bograd. 1982. Paper.

Nicky is a victim of poverty and street life. He commits a burglary and is arrested. EA LA M L

The Bigger Book of Lydia, Margaret Willey. 1983. Paper.

Lydia is small, but her problem is unimportant compared with Michelle's anorexia nervosa. EA LA F

The Boll Weevil Express, P. J. Petersen. 1983. Paper.

Three teenagers run away to San Francisco. PA EA

Center Line, Joyce Sweeney. 1984. Paper.

Five brothers run away from their abusive, alcoholic father. The book's realistic language and sexual encounters are handled with sensitivity. LA *

The Changelings, Jo Sinclair. 1955. Paper.

African Americans unsuccessfully seek housing in a Jewish neighborhood. Judith believes the blacks are the enemy until a girl offers her protection when Judith's status as gang leader is challenged. EA LA F +

The Day They Came to Arrest the Book, Nat Hentoff. 1982. Paper.

Three groups want to have *Huckleberry Finn* removed from the school library: blacks because it is racist, women because it is sexist, and parents because it is immoral. The community becomes polarized over the battle. EA LA +

The Drowning of Stephan Jones, Bette Greene. 1991. Paper.

This powerfully moving novel about family, friendship, love, and homophobia is a mature novel to read and discuss with your adolescents. EA LA *

Everything Is Not Enough, Sandy Asher. 1987. Paper.

This book is about four teenagers' love relationships and the abuse that exists in one of them. LA F

Find a Stranger, Say Good-Bye, Lois Lowry. 1978. Paper.

Natalie is an adopted daughter who feels compelled to seek the identity of her biological parents. EA F

First Blood, David Morrell. 1972. Paper.

A Vietnam veteran comes home scarred by the violence he experienced in the war. This is a good book to discuss with older adolescents. LA

Fiskadoro, Denis Johnson. 1985.

This book is set long after a nuclear holocaust in the last remaining part of the United States. EA LA L

God's Radar, Fran Arrick. 1983. Paper.

A teenager is caught between the fundamentalism of the community and the humanism of her family. EA LA *

Happy Endings Are All Alike, Sandra Scoppettone. 1978. Paper.

Jaret's rape by a disturbed boy leads to her discovery of her lesbianism and a relationship with Peggy. LA F

The Kolokol Papers, Larry Bograd. 1981.

Lev's father, a major civil rights leader in the Soviet Union, is arrested. Lev is left in charge of his family and struggles to get a secret transcript of his father's trial. Although written as a social commentary, the novel has become an interesting work of historical fiction. EA LA + L

Los Alamos Light, Larry Bograd. 1983.

Maggie's father is invited to work as a physicist in Los Alamos in 1943. Secrecy surrounds their lives; the story depicts how different family members handle the tension. EA LA

The Love Bombers, Gloria Miklowitz. 1980. Paper.

Jenna searches for her brother Jeremy, who has joined a group known as the Church of the World. The book attempts to give an objective view of religious cults. EA LA

Maniac Magee, Jerry Spinelli. 1990. Paper.

This Newbery Medal–winning book about a runaway is alter-
nately heartbreaking, heartwarming, and humorous.   PA EA +.
Another Spinelli book on a social issue likely to appeal to
some of the same readers is *Night of the Whale* (1985; paper).
EA LA

A Matter of Principle, Susan Beth Pfeffer. 1982.

High school students print an underground paper, are sus-
pended, and become involved in a legal battle to defend their
First Amendment rights.   LA

Night Kites, M. E. Kerr. 1986. Paper.

A popular young man returns to his conservative hometown
after contracting the HIV virus. The story deals with how he
is treated by his family and those he thought were his
friends.   LA

Nothing but the Truth: A Documentary Novel, Avi. 1991.

Philip wants to run on the high school track team but is unwilling to accept the coaches' good advice. Seemingly unimportant issues escalate into a major controversy when Philip
rebels against other teachers, humming rather than standing at
attention during "The Star-Spangled Banner." In this book Avi
makes it clear that no one wins when conflict is allowed to
escalate.   EA LA

Pride of the Peacock, Stephanie Tolan. 1986.

Whitney is terrified of a nuclear disaster and lashes out at others who do not seem to understand her concern. Eventually
she learns to deal with life more optimistically.   EA + L

Sex Education, Jenny Davis. 1988. Paper.

This novel has an unusual plot dealing with an unusual biology
project in which students are required to care for someone else
for the semester. Livvie and David choose a pregnant neighbor
who is terrorized by her husband.   PA EA F

Simple Gifts, Joanne Greenberg. 1986. Paper.

A government agency wants to turn the Fleurises' rundown farm into a tourist attraction. EA

A Sinless Season, Damon Galgut. 1982.

The story takes place in a reformatory where four boys are involved in a wave of destructive impulses. Violence may make this book inappropriate for less mature readers. LA L

Slake's Limbo, Felice Holman. 1974. Paper.

Thirteen-year-old Aremis is alone in New York and makes his home in the subway. When an accident destroys the world he has built, he finds the courage to launch a life above ground. PA EA * +

Steffie Can't Come Out to Play, Fran Arrick. 1978. Paper.

Steffie runs away to become a model and becomes a prostitute instead. EA LA F *

Summer Smith Begins, Sandy Asher. 1980. Paper.

Terry, who does not like controversy, writes an article for her school newspaper which causes an unexpected uproar. Terry's father defends her editorial against the principal's complaints and wants her to stand up for her rights; her mother disagrees. Terry is caught in the middle. Readers will also enjoy Asher's *Daughters of the Law* (1980, L) and *Missing Pieces* (1984). EA F

Talking in Whispers, James Watson. 1984.

This novel deals with what happens to civil rights in a military dictatorship in Chile. EA LA L

The War Between the Classes, Gloria Miklowitz. 1985. Paper.

A social studies class takes part in the Color Game, a four-week experiment designed to help students understand the damage done by labeling and stereotyping. Miklowitz's other popular books relating to social issues include *After the Bomb* (1985; paper) and *The Day the Senior Class Got Married* (1983; paper). EA

The Wave, Morton Rhue (Todd Strasser). 1981. Paper.

A history teacher uses a teaching method called the Wave to introduce students to what it would be like to live under a fascist government. The experiment backfires when it moves beyond the classroom. EA LA * +

When the Stars Begin to Fall, James Lincoln Collier. 1986. Paper.

Harry sets out to expose a carpet factory that is polluting the river and meets resistance from everyone, including his family. EA LA

Who Is Eddie Leonard?, Harry Mazer. 1993.

Eddie has lived with his grandmother for almost fifteen years. After she dies, he sees what he thinks is his face on a poster of missing children. He sets out to seek his family. PA EA *

The Winchesters, James Lincoln Collier. 1988. Paper.

A strike forces Chris Winchester to choose between his rich family and the people who work in the Winchester Mills. EA

• • • • • •

"Good-Cry" Novels

Handicaps and Illness

Go Ask Alice, Anonymous. 1971. Paper.

This is one of the most popular of all adolescent books, as timely today as when it was written. It is a frank diary of a fifteen-year-old girl's terrifying experiences with drugs. EA LA

I Never Promised You a Rose Garden, Joanne Greenberg (Hannah Green). 1964. Paper.

In this popular book, a young girl journeys back from madness to sanity. EA

Just One Friend, Lynn Hall. 1985.

Dory, age sixteen, has learning disabilities. She tries to stop her

friend from riding in another girl's new car and inadvertently
causes a fatal accident.   EA F *

The Language of Goldfish, Zibby Oneal. 1980. Paper.

Carrie, an upperclass teenager, is beginning to lose her grip on
reality. A suicide attempt puts her in the hospital, where she
gets the help she needs.   EA LA F

Lisa, Bright and Dark, John Neufeld. 1969. Paper.

Lisa is an intelligent teenager on the brink of insanity, but her
parents and teachers refuse to acknowledge her problem. Only
three friends can help Lisa cope with her illness.   EA LA *

The People Therein, Mildred Lee. 1980.

A lame eighteen-year-old Appalachian girl meets and falls in
love with a botanist from Boston.   LA F L

Perdita, Isabelle Holland. 1981. Paper.

Perdita is in an accident and develops amnesia. The author
weaves a mystery around the discovery of every new memory.   PA EA F

Wheels for Walking, Sandra Richmond. 1983. Paper.

A ski weekend turns into tragedy for Sally when she severs her
spinal cord in a car accident. She must adjust to life as a quad-
riplegic. The ending is optimistic.   EA LA F *

Winning, Robin Brancato. 1977. Paper.

A young man's football injury results in permanent paralysis.
The story is told from the perspectives of the young man,
his girlfriend, and his English teacher. The football player
learns that winning involves far more than physical prowess.
EA LA * +

With You & Without You, Ann M. Martin. 1986. Paper.

Liza and her siblings must deal with the knowledge of their
father's disease.   PA EA *

Death

About David, Susan Beth Pfeffer. 1980. Paper.

David murders his adoptive parents and kills himself. Lynn, his friend since childhood, must find out why before she can confront her feelings about him. EA LA *

Close Enough to Touch, Richard Peck. 1981. Paper.

Matt has barely recovered from his mother's death when his girlfriend dies. Though his father and stepmother are loving and supportive, they are unable to understand the depth of his grief. It is not until he meets Margaret that he is able to come to terms with death and life. EA LA *

Dead Bird's Singing, Marc Talbert. 1985. Paper.

Matt must deal with the death of his mother and sister who were killed by a drunk driver. EA

A Formal Feeling, Zibby Oneal. Viking, 1982. Puffin, paper.

Anne is obsessed by the memory of her dead mother. Her obsession, which is more awe at her mother's many talents than love, haunts the rest of Anne's family. EA LA F L

A Ring of Endless Light, Madeleine L'Engle. 1980. Paper.

Vicky struggles with her grandfather's slow death as she learns about life while working with dolphins. EA F * +

Sheila's Dying, Alden R. Carter. 1987. Paper.

This novel is the heartbreaking and heartwarming story of a remarkable friendship. EA LA F L

The Summer Before, Patricia Windsor. 1973. Paper.

Alexandra must come to terms with her best friend's death. Her parents, a friend, and her psychiatrist help her deal with "losing the first person you ever loved." EA F

Sunshine, Norma Klein. 1974. Paper.

Kate has bone cancer but refuses treatment because it might distort her life. The narrative takes the form of a tape-recorded diary from Kate for her daughter. EA LA F *

A Taste of Blackberries, Doris Buchanan Smith. 1973. Paper.

Jamie's best friend is stung by a bee and dies. Jamie blames himself for not doing something to prevent it. At the funeral, Jamie begins to deal with the tragedy and death.   PA EA +

Waiting for Johnny Miracle, Alice Bach. 1980.

One twin sister discovers she has bone cancer; the other is healthy. The novel deals with their attempts to come to terms with this difference and with the emotional impact on the family, life in the pediatric cancer ward, and their struggle to keep life as normal as possible.   EA LA

When the Phone Rang, Harry Mazer. 1985. Paper.

The phone call told the Keller children that their parents had been killed in a plane crash. The story is about how the three teenage children deal with this tragic loss. Another book by Mazer dealing with the theme of being without parents is *Someone's Mother Is Missing* (1990; paper).   EA *

Humor

The Adventures of Huckleberry Finn, Mark Twain, 1884. Paper.

In this classic adventure story, Huck Finn journeys down the Mississippi with Jim, a runaway slave. Their relationship changes and grows with each adventure.   EA LA

The Cat Ate My Gymsuit, Paula Danziger. 1974. Paper.

The first of Danziger's very funny books for adolescents deals with a thirteen-year-old girl who is overweight and lonely. When she joins a fight to help a teacher, she finds friendship and her own identity. Danziger's other books include *Can You Sue Your Parents for Malpractice?* (1979; paper *), *The Divorce Express* (1986; paper *), *Earth to Matthew* (1991; paper), *Make Like a Tree and Leave* (1990; paper), *There's a Bat in Bunk Five* (1980; paper *), *This Place Has No Atmosphere* (1989; paper), *It's an Aardvark-Eat-Turtle World* (1985; paper *), *The Pistachio Prescription* (1978; paper *).   PA EA *

Comedy High, Stephen Manes. 1992.

In this improbable story, a boy transfers to a high school whose curriculum is built around the entertainment industry and whose mascot is a volcano. PA

Discontinued, Julian Thompson. 1985. Paper.

Duncan learns he may be the target of the killer who killed his parents. The plot twists and turns until Duncan suggests that good and bad guys alike might just as well go home. Other wonderfully satirical works by Thompson include *A Band of Angels* (1986, L), *Gypsyworld* (1992), *Herb Seasoning* (1990; paper), and *Simon Pure* (1987; paper). EA LA

Half Nelson, Full Nelson, Bruce Stone. 1985. Paper.

When Nelson's father, a second-rate wrestler, runs away from his wife and young daughter, Nelson and a friend go in search of them to try to restore the family. The characters and story are offbeat and funny. EA LA M

The Heroic Life of Al Capsella, J. Clarke. 1990.

With good humor, Clarke tells the story of Al Capsella, a misfit who comes by it naturally; his eccentric parents, whom Al calls Mr. and Mrs. Capsella and hopes are not really his parents; and a cast of other oddball adults. This Australian novel not only lets readers get to know Al, but also allows them to become friends with the adults in Al's life, who help Al understand that he is not destined to be "normal." EA LA

Losing Joe's Place, Gordon Korman. 1990. Paper.

Korman is a master of satire and put-down. This book, although funny, deals with the serious story of three teenage boys who grow up while working in New York City and living in and taking care of the apartment belonging to the brother of one of them. Other humorous books by Korman include *A Semester in the Life of a Garbage Bag* (1987, L) and *The Zucchini Warriors* (1988; paper). EA M

The Snarkout Boys and the Avocado of Death, Daniel Pinkwater. 1982. Paper.

Winston and Walter, the Snarkout boys, have a series of zany adventures. Readers who enjoy this book also will like *The Snarkout Boys and the Baconburg Horror* (1984; paper).   EA *

The War between the Pitiful Teachers & the Splendid Kids, Stanley Kiesel. 1980. Paper.

This satirical novel is about a school called Scratchland where Skinny Malinky leads the kids in a war against the teachers. *Skinny Malinky Leads the War for Kidness* (1985; paper) is the sequel.   PA EA *

Who Put That Hair in My Toothbrush?, Jerry Spinelli. 1984. Paper.

This is a humorous, heartwarming story of sibling rivalry. Other equally warm and funny Spinelli books include *Space Station Seventh Grade* (1984; paper) and *There's a Girl in my Hammerlock* (1991; paper).   PA * +

Coming-of-Age

Anywhere Else but Here, Bruce Clement. 1980. Paper.

Molly wants to begin a new life. Through determination she succeeds, despite people who attempt to get in the way of her dream.   EA LA F

Behave Yourself, Bethany Brant, Patricia Beatty. 1986.

Bethany, the daughter of a circuit preacher in turn-of-the-century Texas, tries to do the right thing but finds it difficult to be good. The book never moralizes but leads readers to self-awareness through Bethany's example.   PA EA F *

Blowfish Live in the Sea, Paula Fox. 1970. Paper.

Eighteen-year-old Ben is a rebel. Deserted by his father when he was very young, he fights the values of his mother and stepfather by dropping out of school and refusing to look for work. When he receives an unexpected message from his father, he agrees to meet him, but is shocked by the alcoholic person he finds.   LA

Bridges to Cross, Paul Janeczko. 1986.

James is trying to establish his own identity when his mother forces him to attend a strict parochial school. Finally, his mother comes to terms with her son's need to establish a personal ethic. EA M L

Bridge to Terabithia, Katherine Paterson. 1979. Paper.

In this Newbery Medal–winning book, a ten-year-old dreams of being the fastest runner in the fifth grade, but learns that friendship is more important. PA EA +

The Catcher in the Rye, J. D. Salinger. 1951. Paper.

In this classic coming-of-age novel, Holden leaves his prep school in Pennsylvania and goes underground in New York City for three days while he tries to sort out his life. LA

Cat Herself, Mollie Hunter. 1986.

Set in the Scottish countryside in a village of tinkers and travelers, this book about Catrona (Cat), who sets out to establish herself at a time when women are not expected to be heard, can be classified as historical fiction. EA F L

Come Sing, Jimmy Jo, Katherine Paterson. 1985. Paper.

James joins his family's country music singing group, but doesn't want to be different from the other kids at school. PA EA *

Dark but Full of Diamonds, Katie Letcher Lyle. 1981.

Sixteen-year-old Scott is hopelessly in love with his English and drama teacher. When his father and the teacher announce that they plan to be married, Scott gets drunk and treats the people around him badly. His actions cause the teacher and his father to give up their marriage plans, but Scott experiences no victory. EA LA L

A Day No Pigs Would Die, Robert Newton Peck. 1972. Paper.

This is a moving story of life and death on a Vermont farm. Because of the simplicity of the plot and the complexity of the theme, this book can be read and enjoyed by readers of all ages. It is a wonderful book for family sharing. EA +

Downtown, Norma Fox Mazer. 1984. Paper.

Pete's parents leave him with his uncle when they flee to avoid prosecution for a crime. Pete must try to find his own identity without telling anyone who he really is.   EA LA *

Edisto, Padgett Powell. 1984. Paper.

Twelve-year-old Simons attempts to make sense of the black-white world in which he has grown up. This book is for only the most sophisticated adolescent readers.   LA

Far from Shore, Kevin Major. 1981. Paper.

Sixteen-year-old Chris blames his small town and his home for his problems. The story, told from the shifting perspectives of Chris and his friends and family, is about Chris's misbehavior and his slow acceptance of responsibility for his own actions.   EA LA M

Gentlehands, M. E. Kerr. 1978. Paper.

Buddy's world seems to collapse when he falls in love and then discovers that his grandfather was a Nazi war criminal.   EA *

The Girl, Robbie Branscum. 1986.

This autobiographical novel depicts the struggles of growing up in poverty in the Arkansas hills. It realistically portrays sexual abuse and sibling courage. Although the book is written for early adolescents, parents may want to read and discuss it with their children.   PA EA F L

The Green of Me, Patricia Lee Gauch. 1978.

As seventeen-year-old Jennifer is traveling on a train to visit her boyfriend, Chris, she reflects on her childhood and her relationship with Chris.   EA LA F L

Growing Season, Alden R. Carter. 1985.

Rich and his five siblings move during his senior year from the city to the country to start a dairy farm.   EA L

Harry & Hortense at Hormone High, Paul Zindel. 1984. Paper.

Harry and Hortense learn about hero worship from Jason, a schizophrenic who believes he is the reincarnation of Icarus.

When Jason commits suicide, Harry and Hortense learn about the hero within each of them. LA

A House Like a Lotus, Madeleine L'Engle. 1984.

As seventeen-year-old Polly travels through Greece, her reflections on the events of the previous school year allow her to find her own path to understanding and love. EA LA F L

In Summer Light, Zibby Oneal. 1985. Paper.

Kate learns to accept her own abilities and strengths as separate from her exceptionally talented artist father. EA LA F

Is That You, Miss Blue?, M. E. Kerr. 1975. Paper.

Flanders is sent to boarding school, where she learns about cruelty, friendship, and caring. PA EA F * +

Jacob Have I Loved, Katherine Paterson. 1980. Paper.

In this Newbery Medal–winning book, Louise searches for her own identity while fighting jealousy toward her talented, beautiful, and fragile twin. EA F

The Leaving, Lynn Hall. 1980. Paper.

Roxanne graduates from high school and decides that a job in the city is the ticket to happiness. EA LA F

Midnight Hour Encores, Bruce Brooks. 1986. Paper.

Sibilance, a sixteen-year-old who has been raised by her father, sets out to find her mother and discovers the importance of her father's love and support. EA

The Moves Make the Man, Bruce Brooks. 1984. Paper.

Jerome is the first African American student in a high school in the 1950s. The novel tells about his friendship with a troubled young man struggling with his mother's mental illness and his stepfather's antagonism. EA LA *

My Ántonia, Willa Cather. 1918. Paper.

Ántonia, a daughter of immigrants, finds a place for herself on the land and in the community. LA F

Notes for Another Life, Sue Ellen Bridgers. 1981. Paper.

Kevin and Wren must discover their identities while living with their grandparents and struggling to understand their father's mental illness and their mother's desire to live away from her children.   EA LA +

One-Eyed Cat, Paula Fox. 1984. Paper.
Ned must deal with his guilt after injuring a cat with an air rifle.   EA LA

Over the Moon, Elissa Haden Guest. 1986. Paper.
Kate has lived with her aunt since her parents died. When she goes to visit her older sister, she comes to terms with her own identity.   EA LA F

Permanent Connections, Sue Ellen Bridgers. 1987. Paper.
Sixteen-year-old Rob is forced to care for his aunt and grandfather in their Appalachian mountain home. He finds his own identity in the rugged mountains.   EA LA

Portrait of the Artist as a Young Man, James Joyce. 1916. Paper.
This stream-of-consciousness monologue takes Stephen from childhood to early manhood. This classic novel is for very mature adolescent readers.   LA

Prank, Kathryn Lasky. 1984. Paper.
Birdie finds a metaphor for her life in the chipped madonna that stands among the weeds in the front yard.   LA

A Separate Peace, John Knowles. 1960. Paper.
An unspoken rivalry between two friends in a New England prep school mirrors the beginning of World War II. *Peace Breaks Out* (1982; paper) is its long-awaited sequel.   EA LA

A Solitary Blue, Cynthia Voigt. 1983. Paper.
Jeff thinks the solitary blue heron is a good symbol for his life until he learns the importance of his father's love.   EA M +

Summer of My German Soldier, Bette Greene. 1973. Paper.
A Jewish girl feels all alone in her Arkansas town during World War II until she befriends a German prisoner of war. In its

sequel, *Morning Is a Long Time Coming* (1979; paper), Patty searches for the prisoner's parents.   EA LA F * +

Thirty-six Exposures, Kevin Major. 1984.

Lorne searches for himself through the photographs he takes to complete a class project. Readers who enjoy this book should like others by Major, including *Blood Red Ochre* (1989; paper) and *Hold Fast* (1979; paper).   EA LA M

Three Sisters, Norma Fox Mazer. 1986. Paper.

Karen feels overshadowed by her older sisters and nearly destroys her relationship with her family.   EA F

Tiger Eyes, Judy Blume. 1981. Paper.

After her father's murder, Davey meets Wolf, whose father is dying of cancer.   EA LA F *

Travelers, Larry Bograd. 1986.

Jack has built a superman image of his father, who was killed in Vietnam. In learning the truth about his father, he learns much about himself.   EA LA M L

Underneath I'm Different, Ellen Rabinowich. 1983. Paper.

An overweight girl learns to overcome her problems when she meets a fellow student with serious psychological problems. He helps convince her of her own worth and enables her to escape from her mother's overprotection.   EA F *

Up Country, Alden R. Carter. 1989. Paper.

Carl must leave the home of his alcoholic mother in Milwaukee and move to rural Blind River to live with a distant aunt and uncle.   EA LA

Where the Lilies Bloom, Vera Cleaver and Bill Cleaver. 1969. Paper.

Several children are left on their own in the mountains after their father dies. They survive by wild-crafting—collecting plants for medicinal purposes. *Trial Valley* (1987 * + L) is the sequel.   PA EA * +

Yesterday's Daughter, Patricia Calvert. 1986. Paper.

An illegitimate girl meets a photographer whose photographs
teach her to look at her life from a different angle. EA F

Animals

The Bear, William Faulkner. In *Three Famous Short Novels*. 1958.
Paper.
This is a classic hunting story about a search for a legendary
bear, which explores the theme of corruption versus innocence. EA LA

The Black Stallion, Walter Farley. 1944. Paper.
This is the heartwarming story of a boy, a horse, a shipwreck,
and a race. Other books in the series include *Son of the Black
Stallion* (paper), *The Black Stallion and Satan* (paper), and *The
Island Stallion* (paper). PA * +

The Cry of the Crow, Jean Craighead George. 1980. Paper.
The author, who is intimately familiar with animals, tells a
wonderful story about a girl and a crow that mimics hunters.
PA EA +

The Incredible Journey; A Tale of Three Animals, Sheila Burnford.
1961. Paper.
In this story two dogs and a cat make a long homeward
trek. EA +

Julie of the Wolves, Jean Craighead George. 1972. Paper.
This is a Newbery Medal–winning book about a young girl's
struggle to survive on the North Slope of Alaska with the help
of a pack of Arctic wolves. PA EA F * +

King of the Wind, Marguerite Henry. 1948. Paper.
This is the tale of a mute boy's love for a championship
horse. PA +

The Red Pony, John Steinbeck. 1945. Paper.
This is a short, delightful coming-of-age story about a boy and
the death of his beloved pony. PA EA +

Summer of the Monkeys, Wilson Rawls. 1977. Paper.

Jay Berry takes on the task of capturing a tribe of escaped monkeys in the Oklahoma mountains. PA

A Time to Fly Free, Stephanie S. Tolan. 1983. Paper.

A bright but belligerent boy leaves school to work for a man who cares for injured birds. He learns many things from the experience. PA

Watership Down, Richard Adams. 1974. Paper.

This is a fantasy about the breakup of a rabbit warren and the rabbits' search for a new home. Though parts can be shared with the entire family, its length makes it more appropriate for older readers. PA EA +

Where the Red Fern Grows, Wilson Rawls. 1961. Paper.

During the Depression, Billy buys and trains two coon dogs. He wins a gold cup in the annual coon contest and learns about love and trust. PA * +

Historical Fiction

Across Five Aprils, Irene Hunt. 1964. Paper.

Jethro is too young to fight in the Civil War, but he watches his older brothers go off to opposing armies. His parents are stricken by grief and suffering as the neighbors seek vengeance. EA LA +

All Quiet on the Western Front, Erich M. Remarque. 1929. Paper.

A young German soldier experiences the horrors of war in this classic novel about World War I. LA M

Beyond the Divide, Kathryn Lasky. 1983. Paper.

Fourteen-year-old Meribah, to accompany her father on the '49 Gold Rush, leaves her Pennsylvania Amish community. Hardships along the way, including the rape of a friend and the deaths of that friend and her father, lead to Meribah being taken in by the Yahi Indians. PA EA +

The Borning Room, Paul Fleischman. 1991. Paper.

This unusual novel interweaves issues of the Civil War, slavery, resistance to the draft, World War I, women's suffrage, emerging science and medicine, religion, and rituals of birth and death, tied together by the setting of the borning room. Two other interesting historical fiction novels by Fleischman are *Coming-and-Going Men: Four Tales* (1985) and *Saturnalia* (1990; paper).   LA

Cave Under the City, Harry Mazer. 1986. Paper.

During the Depression, Tolley experiences hardships when he must assume responsibility for his five-year-old brother. Mazer also explores the theme of young people alone in *Snow Bound* (1973) and *The Island Keeper* (1981).   EA *

The Clan of the Cave Bear, Jean Auel. 1980. Paper.

The first and best of Auel's prehistoric series is appropriate for young readers. A Cro-Magnon girl is adopted by a tribe of Neanderthals and struggles to subdue her abilities while growing up in a mystical, male-dominated society.   LA F

Fallen Angels, Walter Dean Myers. 1988. Paper.

Richie Perry is seventeen in 1967 and is on his way to Vietnam. He is sure the war is over and his bad knee will keep him out of combat. He sees the army as his ticket to college to fulfill his dream of writing like James Baldwin. He meets Peewee Gates on the flight over, and they remain side-by-side throughout combat. They not only endure the enemy, but also racism within the army.   LA *

The Fighting Ground, Avi. 1984. Paper.

In 1778, thirteen-year-old Jonathan joins the American militia against his father's wishes. Instead of glory, he experiences pain, brutality, and death. Readers who enjoy this book should also read *The True Confessions of Charlotte Doyle* (1990; paper).   EA +

Forbidden City: A Novel of Modern China, William Bell. 1990. Paper.

This novel focuses on a relatively recent event in history: the Tianamen Square student uprising.   LA

Frontier Wolf, Rosemary Sutcliff. 1981.

In fourth-century Britain, Centurion Alexios is disgraced and sent to an outpost on the Firth of Forth. His skill and courage redeem his reputation as a Roman commander.   EA + L

I Am Rosemarie, Marietta D. Moskin. 1972.

In this autobiographical novel, the author catalogs the human triumphs during the Holocaust. Rosemarie spends her early teenage years hiding in a series of German settlement camps. She shares these years with her family and remains grateful and optimistic throughout.   PA EA LA F L

I Be Somebody, Hadley Irwin. 1984. Paper.

Rap and other black citizens are hoodwinked into buying seats on the freedom train to Athabasca in Canada during this little-known episode in African American history.   PA EA * +

Johnny Tremain, Esther Forbes. 1943. Paper.

In this classic work, Johnny dreams of becoming a silversmith, but his dreams are dashed when his right hand is burned and crippled. As he seeks a new way of life he is led into the intrigue and adventure of the Boston Tea Party.   PA +

Journey to America, Sonia Leviton. 1970. Paper.

The Platts, a Jewish family fleeing Nazi Germany, are separated during their escape and finally reunited in New York.   PA EA

Jump Ship to Freedom, James L. Collier and Christopher Collier. 1981. Paper.

Daniel, the son of a slave, is willed Continental notes to secure his freedom following the Revolution. *War Comes to Willy Freeman* (1987; paper) and *Who Is Carrie?* (1984; paper) are a part of the same series.   PA +

The Last Mission, Harry Mazer. 1979. Paper.

Loosely based on an incident in the author's own life, this book is about a teenager who enlists in the World War II Army Air Corps using his brother's birth certificate as proof of age. He expects to find glory in war, but finds horror and hardship instead.   EA LA M *

The Massacre at Fall Creek, Jessamyn West. 1975. Paper.

This is the story of the trial following the massacre of Indians by five white men. LA

My Brother Sam Is Dead, James L. Collier and Christopher Collier. 1974. Paper.

A sixteen-year-old joins the Continental Army against his parents' wishes. The other books in the trilogy, *The Bloody Country* (1977; paper) and *The Winter Hero* (1978; paper), deal respectively with the land dispute between Connecticut and Pennsylvania and Shays's Rebellion. PA +

Nightjohn, Gary Paulsen. 1993.

This is an exciting, disturbing tale about a slave who escaped to the North. It is narrated by a twelve-year-old slave girl. PA EA

No Hero for the Kaiser, Rudolf Frank. 1931. Paper.

Originally published in German, this book is about the effects of World War I on a young hero who, along with his dog, becomes part of an invading German battery after his Polish village is devastated. LA M

Prairie Songs, Pam Conrad. 1985. Paper.

Louisa gains a better understanding of prairie life by contrasting the character and plain beauty of her mother with the frail loveliness of the new doctor's wife. Readers who enjoy this book should also enjoy Conrad's *My Daniel* (1989). PA EA

Ride into Morning: The Story of Tempe Wick, Ann Rinaldi. 1991.

Told from the female perspective, this story is based on the Revolutionary War legend of Tempe Wick, who hides her horse in the house overnight so the soldiers won't steal him. Other interesting works of historical fiction by Rinaldi include *A Break with Charity: A Story about the Salem Witch Trials* (1992), *Time Enough for Drums* (1986; paper), and *Wolf by the Ears* (1991). PA EA F

The Road to Damietta, Scott O'Dell. 1985.

This novel, set in a thirteenth-century Italian village, is the story of a young girl whose love for Francis causes her to join him on the Fifth Crusade. Other popular historical fiction by O'Dell includes *Island of the Blue Dolphins* (1960; paper), *Carlotta* (1977; paper), *Sarah Bishop* (1980; paper), *The Serpent Never Sleeps* (1980; paper), and *Black Star, Bright Dawn* (1988; paper). PA EA F +

The Samurai's Tale, Erik Christian Haugaard. 1984. Paper.

The son of a samurai is orphaned and captured by powerful enemies of his father. He becomes a servant and must work his way up to Samurai. PA

The Slave Dancer, Paula Fox. 1973. Paper.

Jesse is kidnapped and taken aboard a slave ship where he is forced to play his fife so that the slaves will dance and not lose their physical condition. He struggles with conflicting emotions of compassion and hate. PA EA +

Walking up a Rainbow, Theodore Taylor. 1986. Paper.

A fourteen-year-old orphan fights to save her California sheep ranch. PA EA +

The Wall, John Hersey. 1961. Paper.

The Jews of the Warsaw ghetto stand up against their oppressors. LA

The Witch of Blackbird Pond, Elizabeth George Speare. 1958. Paper.

The niece of a family in colonial Connecticut befriends the witch of Blackbird Pond and learns of the colonists' cruelty. PA EA +

You Never Knew Her As I Did!, Mollie Hunter. 1981.

In this novel based on the imprisonment of Mary, Queen of Scots, a seventeen-year-old devises a plan for her escape. PA EA + L

. . . . .
Multicultural

African American Heroes

The Autobiography of Miss Jane Pittman, Ernest Gaines. 1971.
Paper.

This fictional account of Jane Pittman, who was born a slave
and freed soon after the Civil War, takes readers from the Civil
War to the civil rights movement of the 1960s.   EA LA +

Beloved, Toni Morrison. 1987. Paper.

In this contemporary classic, the story of three generations of
women, Morrison creates a ghost story, a mystery, and a work
of historical fiction. The complex storyline vividly shows how
African Americans were treated before, during, and immediately following the Civil War.   LA

Freedom Road, Howard Fast. 1969.

This historic novel, set in the Reconstruction South and based
on facts and events of this period, is about a former slave who
dreams of beginning a community where blacks and whites
can live together.   EA LA L

The Friends, Rosa Guy. 1973. Paper.

A lonely girl in Harlem learns that appearances are not as important as friendship. In the sequel, *Edith Jackson* (1978), Edith
tries to keep her family together after the death of her parents.   EA F *

A Gathering of Old Men, Ernest Gaines. 1983. Paper.

After a white man feared by blacks is killed, a white woman
and a dozen old black men claim to have killed him. They are
all protecting something important to them.   LA

A Hero Ain't Nothin' but a Sandwich, Alice Childress. 1973. Paper.

This story of a thirteen-year-old drug user is told from his own
perspective as well as those of his mother, grandmother, stepfather, teachers, and friends.   EA LA *

If Beale Street Could Talk, James Baldwin. 1974. Paper.

In this masterful book a young man is framed and jailed while he and his girlfriend are supported by a loyal family. LA

Invisible Man, Ralph Ellison. 1951. Paper.

A nameless hero learns that his search for identity involves confrontation with whites and blacks. This is a classic story of innocence and answers. LA

Ludell's New York Time, Brenda Wilkinson. 1980.

In this sequel to *Ludell* (1975; paper) and *Ludell and Willie* (1977; paper), Ludell has left her rural Georgia home after her grandmother's death. She finds that New York offers nothing but dead-end jobs and wants to go home to marry Willie. EA LA F * L

M.C. Higgins, the Great, Virginia Hamilton. 1974. Paper.

This is a lyrical story about a boy whose only special talent is sitting atop a flagpole. He learns that life is far more than sitting and watching the world go by. Readers who enjoy this book are likely to enjoy *A Little Love* (1984, L) and *A White Romance* (1987; paper), also by Hamilton. EA LA

Mojo and the Russians, Walter Dean Myers. 1977.

Dean believes Drusilla has placed a voodoo spell on him, and his gang devises a plan to "unfix" him from the spell. In the process they meet the "Russian spy." L. *The Young Landlords* (1979; paper) follows the same cast of humorous characters on another endeavor. A hilarious mystery for young readers is *The Mouse Rap* (1990; paper). Myers's other humorous tales of inner-city African American youth include *Fast Sam, Cool Clyde, and Stuff* (1975; paper), *Me, Mop and the Moondance Kid* (1988; paper), and *Mop, Moondance, and the Nagasaki Knights* (1992). PA EA M * +

The Original Colored House of David, Martin Quigley. 1981.

In the Midwest in the late 1920s, Timmy seeks a chance to prove his manliness and athletic skill. EA M L

Rainbow Jordan, Alice Childress. 1981. Paper.

In this moving story about three black women, Rainbow, fourteen, is frequently left alone by her mother. Because of her mother's neglect, she meets Miss Josephine, a loving older woman sent by Social Services when Rainbow is left alone for several days.   EA F

Roll of Thunder, Hear My Cry, Mildred Taylor. 1976. Paper.

A black family struggles to maintain dignity and self-respect in the poverty of the 1930s in Mississippi. This book and its sequel, *Let the Circle Be Unbroken* (1981; paper), contrast family love with the prejudice that pervades the community. *The Road to Memphis* (1990; paper) continues the family saga. *Song of the Trees* is another Taylor book set in rural Mississippi (1975; paper).   EA LA +

This Strange New Feeling, Julius Lester. 1982. Paper.

Three stories are tied together by a common plot in which African Americans attempt to gain freedom during the antebellum period.   EA LA

To Kill a Mockingbird, Harper Lee. 1961. Paper.

Life in a small Alabama town is seen through the eyes of a young girl who observes her father's courtroom defense of a black man accused of raping a white woman.   EA LA +

When the Nightingale Sings, Joyce Carol Thomas. 1992.

This lyrical novel takes place in a conservative, religious African American community. Marigold attempts to escape the present and learn about the past by singing and writing her own songs.   EA F +

Words by Heart, Ouida Sebestyen. 1979. Paper.

In the early 1900s, prejudice against blacks in the West makes it difficult for Lena Sills to find a home. Through her family's love she finds a place for herself.   EA F * +

Ethnic Heroes

Chernowitz!, Fran Arrick. 1981. Paper.

Cherno tries to ignore the anti-Semitic remarks of the class bully. Action by his parents and the principal brings the prejudice into the open. EA

Child of the Owl, Laurence Yep. 1977. Paper.

Casey, a Chinese-American girl, has lived a nomadic life with her gambler father. When her father is hospitalized and she is sent to stay with her grandmother, she begins to search for her identity. EA +

The Chosen, Chaim Potok. 1967. Paper.

A young Hasidic Jew searches for his identity in New York City. Another Potok book on a similar topic is *My Name is Asher Lev* (1972; paper). LA

The Crossing, Gary Paulsen. 1987. Paper.

Manuel Bustos is a fourteen-year-old orphan in a Mexican border town. The sergeant he meets decides not to turn Manny over to the border patrol even though Manny has attempted to steal the sergeant's wallet. From this and other chance meetings, their lives are bound in the novel's exciting climax. The suspenseful sequel to this novel is *Sentries* (1986; paper). Other equally exciting books by Paulsen include *Canyons* (1990; paper) and *The Night the White Deer Died* (1990; paper). EA LA *

Davita's Harp, Chaim Potok. 1985. Paper.

Davita lives with her politically involved parents in New York City in the 1930s and 1940s. Her parents have defied their religious heritage, and she must search for hers. LA F

Eyes of Darkness, Jamake Highwater. 1985.

This book, based on the true story of a Santee Indian physician at the time of the Wounded Knee massacre, is the story of a sensitive young man who has dedicated himself to bringing two cultures together. EA LA +

Ganesh, Malcolm J. Bosse. 1981.

Ganesh moves to the rural American Midwest when his father dies in India. At first he is isolated from other young people who consider his knowledge of yoga and Indian philosophies strange. EA

I Wear the Morning Star, Jamake Highwater. 1986.

This third book in the "Ghost Horse Cycle" is the story of Sitko, a young First American searching for his identity. Sitko is an artist who paints the stories told to him by his grandmother. The other two books in the cycle are *Legend Days* (1984) and *The Ceremony of Innocence* (1985). PA EA LA +

Mountain Light, Laurence Yep. 1985.

The setting for this novel is the 1855 rebellion in China. Squeaky thinks he is a coward and becomes a clown, a trait that serves him well against his enemies. When he flees China he discovers that the feuds still exist in America. PA EA + L

The Return, Sonia Levitin. 1987. Paper.

A black Ethiopian Jewish girl leaves her mountain homeland with her brother and younger sister to fulfill her dream of going to the promised land called Israel. PA EA

The Shadow Brothers, A. E. Cannon. 1990.

This novel is about modern Native Americans and their need to recognize and learn about their heritage and identity as they try to be assimilated in white society. Henry Yazzie is a Navaho sent by his father to live with a white middle-class family. EA LA

When the Legends Die, Hal Borland. 1963. Paper.

Thomas punishes the rodeo horse he rides until a terrible accident sends him back to the mountains of his Indian youth. EA

Mystery

The Arm of the Starfish, Madeleine L'Engle. 1965. Paper.

Adam expects to spend a quiet summer working for a marine biologist but instead becomes involved in an international mystery. EA +

The Callender Papers, Cynthia Voigt. 1983. Paper.

In this gothic novel, Jean plans to spend her summer cataloging family papers in the old Callender home. She soon realizes the papers contain the key to the family mystery. EA

Down a Dark Hall, Lois Duncan. 1974. Paper.

In this gothic romance about ESP, four girls become prisoners in an exclusive girls' school. They realize why they were selected and how vulnerable they are. EA F *

Dragons in the Waters, Madeleine L'Engle. 1976. Paper.

Combining murder, politics, and history to create suspense, this novel is full of information on Venezuela, oil refining, and science. EA LA +

Fell, M. E. Kerr. 1987. Paper.

This is the first book of a series of mysteries with an unlikely detective. The protagonist is a likable teenage sleuth and preppie gourmet who solves mysteries by taking on the exclusive Gardner School. Fans of Kerr, humor, and mystery will enjoy this, as well as *Fell Back* (1989; paper) and *Fell Down* (1991; paper). PA EA * +

Footsteps: A Novel, Leon Garfield. 1980.

The setting for this eighteenth-century mystery is William's father's bedroom. William attempts to fulfill his father's deathbed wish to find a man he swindled. EA

The Man in the Woods, Rosemary Wells. 1984. Paper.

Helen, a reporter for her school paper, finds her life threatened after she witnesses a vicious crime. Her personal integrity and the help of a teenage boy keep her on the case until it is solved. EA

The Seance, Joan Lowery Nixon. 1980. Paper.

Sara, who lives with Lauren and her family, disappears after a seance and is presumed dead. When a second teenager is murdered, Lauren is sure she will be next. Other popular mystery/suspense books by Nixon include *Candidate for Murder* (1991; paper), *Caught in the Act* (1988; paper), *The Kidnapping of Christina Lattimore* (1979; paper), *The Weekend Was Murder!* (1992; paper), and *The Name of the Game Was Murder* (1993). EA

Sirens and Spies, Janet Taylor Lisle. 1985. Paper.

Mary and Elsie become involved in a mystery surrounding their violin teacher, who has a mysterious past in occupied France during World War II. EA F

Sweet Whispers, Brother Rush, Virginia Hamilton. 1982. Paper.

Is Brother Rush really a ghost of a fifteen-year-old learning to deal with her family's problems? This mystery is a worthwhile challenge for good readers. Also try *The Mystery of Drear House* (1987; paper) and *The House of Dies Drear* (1968; paper). EA +

Tales of a Dead King, Walter Dean Myers. 1983.

There are many mysteries in this entertaining tale: a dead snake in a hotel room, a dagger whistling through the air, a missing archaeologist, and a lost treasure. PA * L

The Young Unicorns, Madeleine L'Engle. 1968.

A sinister gang of youths plots to destroy a former member and the blind musician he tutors. EA + L

You'll Never Guess the End, Barbara Wersba. 1992.

The male protagonist is ignored by his parents and loves the Metropolitan Museum of Art and Central Park. The plot involves the kidnapping of his older brother's ex-girlfriend. PA

Suspense

After the First Death, Robert Cormier. 1979. Paper.

A school bus is hijacked by an Arab terrorist, whom readers come to know and understand. The terrifying climax is also thought provoking. EA LA

And Nobody Knew They Were There, Otto Salassi. 1984.

Jakey and his cousin attempt to solve a mystery that grownups cannot. During the course of the story they stalk an elusive prey and survive by their wits. PA EA M * + L

Are You In the House Alone?, Richard Peck. 1976. Paper.

A young girl receives anonymous phone calls and obscene letters, then is raped by someone she knows. EA LA *

Brothers of the Heart, Joan Blos. 1985. Paper.

Fourteen-year-old, handicapped Shem runs away from home and joins a trading expedition. He finds himself alone and lost as winter approaches. Readers who enjoy this book should also enjoy *A Gathering of Days: A New England Girl's Journal* (1979; paper). PA EA F

The Bumblebee Flies Anyway, Robert Cormier. 1983. Paper.

In this psychological thriller, a sixteen-year-old becomes an experimental subject in a hospital treating the chronically ill. EA LA

Crime and Punishment, Fyodor Dostoyevsky. 1866. Paper.

A Russian student who commits robbery and murder is hounded by his own guilt and by a suspicious police inspector. LA

The Executioner, Jay Bennett. 1982. Paper.

Bruce recalls the car accident he caused that killed his friend. His reflection makes him realize that someone is out to kill him. EA *

Fade, Robert Cormier. 1988. Paper.

Thirteen-year-old Paul Moreaux learns that he possesses a

haunting secret with terrifying responsibilities—he can fade from the visible to the invisible world.   EA

Frankenstein, Mary Shelley. 1818. Paper.

A young scientist creates a monster who wreaks havoc and destroys himself.   LA

Hatchet, Gary Paulsen. 1987. Paper.

This book chronicles Brian's survival in the Canadian wilderness after a plane crash. Many young male readers consider it the best book they have ever read. Once they have read it, they have to read its sequel, *The River* (1991). Another Paulsen book that male readers are guaranteed to enjoy is *Tracker* (1984; paper), about tracking deer.   EA M *

I Am the Cheese, Robert Cormier. 1977. Paper.

Adam sets out on a bicycle trip to find his hospitalized father. Throughout the book the reader learns the horrifying secrets shared by Adam and his family.   EA LA

Killing Mr. Griffin, Lois Duncan. 1978. Paper.

A group of high school students set out to scare a strict high school English teacher, but their prank turns into horror. EA * +

Locked in Time, Lois Duncan. 1985. Paper.

Nore's mother dies and Nore goes to live with her father and stepfamily. She soon realizes that a dream in which her mother warns that Nore and her father are in danger is more than her resentment toward her father's remarriage.   EA

Nobody Else Can Walk It for You, P. J. Petersen. 1982. Paper.

In this first-rate adventure story, a strong young woman is responsible for getting a group of teenagers (including several boys) to safety after they're lost on a hike.   EA

On the Edge, Gillian Cross. 1985. Paper.

Tug Shakespeare, son of a prominent London journalist, is kidnapped by a terrorist group attempting to destroy the nuclear family. British writer Cross has written many other books that readers are likely to enjoy. In *Born of the Sun* (1984; paper), Paula is mysteriously withdrawn from boarding school to go with her family on an exploratory expedition into South America. *The Dark behind the Curtain* (1982; paper) is a tale of good versus evil that is set during a secondary school's play production of *Sweeney Todd*. Two other good suspense novels by Cross are *A Map of Nowhere* (1989) and *Roscoe's Leap* (1987; paper). EA

Pursuit, Michael French. 1982. Paper.

A hiking trip in an isolated area ends in a clash of wills among the four hikers. EA LA

A Rumor of Otters, Deborah Savage. 1986.

Alexa lives on an isolated sheep station in New Zealand. She leaves home to search for otters. EA F

Shadow on the Snow, Bill Wallace. 1985.

A city boy moves to the country and learns to fish, explore the wilds, and ride horses. These new skills prepare him for a rescue mission during a blizzard. PA EA M

The Shining, Stephen King. 1978. Paper.

The Torrance family, including five-year-old Daniel who has ESP, must fight demonic forces in the hotel for which they are caretakers. LA

Sweet Friday Island, Theodore Taylor. 1984. Paper.

On a trip to a Mexican island, Peg and her father discover that a madman is attempting to kill them (L). Two other popular books by Taylor, set in the Caribbean, are *The Cay* (1960; paper) and its prequel/sequel *Timothy of the Cay* (1993). EA

To Be a Killer, Jay Bennett. 1985. Paper.

Paul considers killing his chemistry teacher after the teacher catches him stealing a copy of the final exam. Finally he reaches for help instead (L). Other good books by Bennett that are likely to appeal to the same readers include *The Dark Corridor* (1988; paper), *The Haunted One* (1987; paper), and *The Long Black Coat* (1973; L). EA *

The Truth Trap, Frances Miller. 1980. Paper.

Matt is a suspect in the murder of his deaf sister. He is befriended by a detective who believes he is innocent. Readers interested in Matt's problems may want to read *Aren't You the One Who—?* (1983; paper), *Losers and Winners* (1986; L), and *Cutting Loose* (1991; paper). EA

We All Fall Down, Robert Cormier. 1991.

Three lives meet in violent confrontation. Buddy is an alcoholic adolescent who trashes a house and attacks a fourteen-year-old girl; Jane is the girl's older sister and moral focus of the novel; and "The Avenger" witnesses the attack and seeks revenge. LA

Wilderness Peril, Thomas Dygard. 1985. Paper.

On a canoe trip in Minnesota, Todd and Mike find money left by a hijacker. They realize they must be gone before he returns. EA LA M

The Wolves of Willoughby Chase, Joan Aiken. 1962. Paper.

In this winner of the Lewis Carroll Shelf Award, two cousins are left in the care of an evil governess in a nineteenth-century house. Its sequel, *Black Hearts in Battersea* (1964; paper), has even more elements of a suspense story: wolves, a kidnapping, a long-lost heir, a bomb plot, the London underworld, and a tragic death. A second sequel, *Nightbirds on Nantucket* (1981; paper), is also an exciting read (PA EA +). Readers of these books are also likely to enjoy *Died on a Rainy Sunday* (1988; paper) and *Nightfall* (1969; paper). PA EA

Love and Romance

Acts of Love, Maureen Daly. 1986. Paper.

Parents and grandparents of young adults may remember reading Daly's first novel, *Seventeenth Summer* (1942; paper *). In Daly's second novel for young adults, Henrietta deals with changes in her hometown while developing a romantic interest in a mysterious young man with a past tied to her mother. Female readers are also likely to enjoy Daly's *First a Dream* (1990; paper).   EA F *

Beginners' Love, Norma Klein. 1982. Paper.

Joel is shy, while Lela is aggressive. Their relationship progresses into the first sexual encounter for both of them. EA LA F *

Bright Days, Stupid Nights, Norma Fox Mazer and Harry Mazer. 1992. Paper.

Two well-known young adult authors teamed up to write this summer romance about four troubled teenagers.   EA

Cecile, Janine Boissard. 1988. Paper.

This is the love story of a girl from a closely knit, middle-class French family who loses her innocence and comes to terms with love. An earlier novel by this French writer, *A Matter of Feeling* (1979), is another sensitively written romance about Pauline's first love with an artist nearly twice her age. EA LA F

Cloudy-Bright, John Rowe Townsend. 1984.

Sam thinks he likes Jenny because she has the camera he needs to win the photography contest, but he soon realizes that it's more than her camera he's interested in.   EA LA L

A Farewell to Arms, Ernest Hemingway. 1920. Paper.

This love story between an English nurse and a wounded American ambulance driver is set against the backdrop of the Italian campaign in World War I.   LA

The Fat Girl, Marilyn Sachs. 1984. Paper.

Jeff and Norma, the beautiful people, are more than attracted to one another. But when Jeff makes two-hundred-pound Ellen cry, his revulsion turns to fascination and he sets about transforming her.   PA EA F

Finding David Delores, Margaret Willey. 1986.

Arly is obsessed with David and finally meets him, but she learns more about herself and the value of friendship than love.   EA F L

The Haunting of Safekeep, Eve Bunting. 1985.

This book weaves together a love story and a ghost story. To qualify for a summer caretaking job, Sara and Dev agree to become a couple. They soon discover the ghost of Safe-keep.   EA F +

Hey Kid! Does She Love Me?, Harry Mazer. 1984. Paper.

An eighteen-year-old boy in love with a twenty-year-old woman with a baby postpones his move to California to spend the summer with them. Another book dealing with a similar topic from a male's perspective is *The Girl of His Dreams* (1987; paper), which introduces a protagonist who appeared earlier in *The War on Villa Street* (1978; paper). Harry Mazer's romances are unique in that they appeal to male as well as female readers.   EA *

I Stay Near You, M. E. Kerr. 1985.

This romance novel spans three generations tied together by a ring passed from one generation to the next.   EA LA F

The Love Letters of J. Timothy Owens, Constance Greene. 1986. Paper.

Tim finds an old trunk filled with love letters written by famous people. Inspired by the beauty of their language, he decides to write some of his own and send them to Sophie, who is unaware of Tim and is convinced someone is sending her dirty letters.   EA

Motown and Didi: A Love Story, Walter Dean Myers. 1984. Paper.

Didi and Motown fall in love while trying to save Didi's brother from drug addiction.   EA *

My Love, My Love, or the Peasant Girl, Rosa Guy. 1985. Paper.

In this tragic romance, a beautiful black orphan falls in love with a wealthy creole.   EA LA

Orfe, Cynthia Voigt. 1992.

This award-winning writer for young adults writes a compelling romance based on the Orpheus myth.   EA LA *

Romeo and Juliet, William Shakespeare. Paper.

Perhaps the first great adolescent romance, this play about the classical conflict between parents and young lovers is as relevant today as in Shakespeare's time.   EA LA +

Sugar Blue, Vera Cleaver. 1984. Paper.

This is not a romance but a love story about an eleven-year-old girl who takes care of her four-year-old niece.   PA F +

Up in Seth's Room, Norma Fox Mazer. 1979. Paper.

Seth is ready for a sexual relationship, but Finn is not. *Someone to Love* (1983) is another recommended romance by Mazer.   LA F *

What If They Saw Me Now?, Jean Ure. 1984.

Jamie inadvertently becomes a ballet star when he reluctantly agrees to take the place of an injured dancer. He enjoys dancing, but does not want his friends to see him in tights.   EA

When We First Met, Norma Fox Mazer. 1982. Paper.

Jenny falls in love but is horrified to discover that her boyfriend's mother is the drunk driver who killed her sister two years earlier. They develop a relationship without their families' knowledge, but feel guilty about their secretiveness.   EA LA F *

Wuthering Heights, Emily Brontë. 1847. Paper.

This classic British romance depicting the tormented love of Heathcliff and Catherine is set on the rugged moors of the north of England.   LA

Fantasy

Animal Farm, George Orwell. 1954. Paper.

This fantasy/satire is the tale of rebellious animals who attempt to create a society based on equality. LA

The Beginning Place, Ursula K. LeGuin. 1980.

Two alienated teenagers discover the fantasy world of Tembreabrezi while trying to escape from the real world. There they confront their personal problems, fears, and frustrations. LA

The Black Cauldron, Lloyd Alexander. 1965. Paper.

This first book in the "Prydain Chronicles" is an excellent fantasy-quest book that can be read by readers as young as nine or ten years of age, and enjoyed, on a more advanced level, by older readers. The chronicle, based on Welsh legend and myth, is about Taran and his search for his true identity. The chronicles also include *The Book of Three, The Castle of Llyr, The High King*, and *Taran Wanderer* (1964–68; paper) PA EA LA +. Although easy to read, the books create such a complex world that an encyclopedia-like reference guide, *The Prydain Companion: A Reference Guide to Lloyd Alexander's Prydain Chronicles*, written by Michael O. Tunnell (1989), has been published. This source catalogs each character, object, place, and major theme of the novels. A pronunciation guide for Welsh words is included. EA LA

Dragon's Blood, Jane Yolen. 1982. Paper.

In this tale of dragon stealing, training, and fighting, Jakkin is aided by a young girl who becomes his first love. The sequels, *Heart's Blood* (1984; paper * +) and *A Sending of Dragons* (1987; paper), tell us more of the adventures of Jakkin, who is now a young Dragon Master. PA * +

The Darkangel, Meredith Ann Pierce. 1982. Paper.

The Darkangel is a vampire who kidnaps Eoduin to make her his thirteenth bride. When Aeriel seeks to free the wives, she is kidnapped herself, and her growing attachment to the vampire makes it difficult to achieve her goal (L). *A Gathering of Gargoyles* (1984; paper) is the second book of the trilogy in which Aeriel travels to a strange land in search of the answer to a riddle.   EA LA

Dragon of the Lost Sea, Laurence Yep. 1982.

This tale is based loosely on a Chinese myth about the efforts of the shape-changing dragon Shimmer to restore her clan's traditional home.   PA EA

The Flight of the Cassowary, John LeVert. 1986.

John metamorphoses into rats and horses after he begins talking to Ken, a neighborhood dog. In this fantasy, John does not totally leave his real world, and this causes problems for him.   EA LA

The Hero and the Crown, Robin McKinley. 1984. Paper.

Aerin is a strong female heroine who takes on dragon killing when her father refuses to let her ride into battle with the warriors. The fact that she is a motherless misfit princess should appeal to many adolescent girls. Readers who enjoy this tale may also enjoy its prequel, *The Blue Sword* (1982; paper).   EA F

The Left Hand of Darkness, Ursula K. LeGuin. 1976. Paper.

This book takes place in a technologically primitive world in which Ali must face a hostile climate, a contentious government, and his own sexuality.   EA

The Legend of Tarik, Walter Dean Myers. 1981. Paper.

This unusual story is about a black teenage hero who avenges his family's slaughter.   EA

The Lion, the Witch, and the Wardrobe, C. S. Lewis. 1950. Paper.

This classic fantasy, composed as a Christian metaphor, catalogs four children's adventures in the land of Narnia. The six other Narnia tales for young readers who enjoy this first adventure are *Prince Caspian: The Return to Narnia* (1951; paper),

The Voyage of the "Dawn Treader" (1952; paper), *The Silver Chair* (1953; paper), *The Horse and His Boy* (1954; paper), *The Magician's Nephew* (1955; paper), and *The Last Battle* (1965; paper).   PA +

The Lord of the Rings, J. R. R. Tolkien. 1954. Paper.

This epic fantasy trilogy, written for adults, is loved by many older adolescents. Middle Earth becomes the battleground between good and evil as Frodo struggles to destroy the ring and the evil it represents. The other two books in the trilogy are *The Fellowship of the Ring* (1954; paper) and *The Return of the King* (1954; paper).   MA LA

Moreta: Dragon Lady of Pern, Anne McCaffrey. 1983. Paper.

This book explores the planet of Pern (as do six earlier overlapping books in the "Dragonriders of Pern" series), a land in which dragons and their telepathic riders protect the world from deadly silver threads. The books have realistic, earthy characters.   EA F

The Shadow Guests, Joan Aiken. 1980. Paper.

In this cross between fantasy and science fiction, Aiken explores Einstein's theory of relativity, parapsychology, and mysticism to allow Cosmo to encounter three of his ancestors just before they fall victim to a curse.   EA LA

Westmark, Lloyd Alexander. 1981. Paper.

In this first book of the "Westmark Trilogy"—*The Kestral* (1982; paper) and *The Beggar Queen* (1984; paper) are the two others—Theo is forced to leave town because of a murder he thinks he committed. He becomes involved with a medicine showman, a dwarf, a beautiful girl, and Cabbarus, who is influencing the King against him.   PA +

The Wizard of Earthsea, Ursula K. LeGuin. 1968. Paper.

In this first of Leguin's "Earthsea Cycle," Ged must master the monster within himself by facing and defeating the gebbeth from the other world. Ged continues his fight against evil in the next three books: *The Tombs of Atuan* (1971; paper), *The Farthest Shore* (1972; paper), and *Tehanu: The Last Book of Earthsea* (1990; paper).   EA +

A Wrinkle in Time, Madeleine L'Engle. 1962. Paper.

In this first book of L'Engle's "Time Trilogy," three young people transcend time to rescue their father. *A Wind in the Door* (1973; paper) and *A Swiftly Tilting Planet* (1978; paper) are the sequels. All three books are filled with science, the supernatural, and religion. Readers who loved these fantasies may want to continue to follow the lives of the Murrys and O'Keefes of the next generation in *An Acceptable Time* (1989; paper). PA EA +

Folklore, Legend, Myth, and Religion

The Beast, Jonathan Fast. 1981. Paper.

In this contemporary version of the traditional tale of "Beauty and the Beast," Beauty is a movie actress and Beast is a former chemical company director, critically injured and badly scarred in an unsuccessful suicide attempt.   EA LA F +

Beauty: A Retelling of the Story of Beauty and the Beast, Robin McKinley. 1978. Paper.

This is a traditional but much expanded retelling of the classic fairy tale.   PA EA LA F +

Fair Day and Another Step Begun, Katie Letcher Lyle. 1974.

This contemporary novel is based on the "Childe Waters" English ballad. Ellen, pregnant by John, is determined to keep the child and marry John. He is equally determined to abandon her and the child.   EA LA F L

The Hunchback of Notre Dame, Victor Hugo, adapted by Diane Stewart. 1981.

This is among the best of the retellings of this classic tale; illustrations are included.   EA

The Magical Adventures of Pretty Pearl, Virginia Hamilton. 1983. Paper.

Hamilton combines American and African legend and folklore to create a story of Pretty Pearl, a god child from Mount Kenya who convinces her brother and best god to take her to live among the humans. After flying to America as an albatross, Pretty Pearl assumes the shape of a human child and begins her quest to help free blacks.   PA EA

The Maid of the North: Feminist Folktales from around the World, Ethel Johnston Phelps. 1982.

These twenty-one tales from many countries have ingenious, determined heroines.   EA LA F

The Pearl, John Steinbeck. 1947. Paper.

Steinbeck retells an old Mexican legend, embellishing it with wonderful details and exciting adventure. The plot line can be understood by preadolescents and the themes appreciated by late adolescents. This American classic shouldn't be missed.   PA EA LA +

The Road to Camlann: The Death of King Arthur, Rosemary Sutcliff. 1982.

This is one of the best retellings of Arthurian legend for young adults (L). The other books in the trilogy are *The Sword and the Circle* (1981) and *The Light Beyond the Forest* (1980, L).   PA EA +

Seven Daughters and Seven Sons, Barbara Cohen and Bahija Lovejoy. 1982.

In this is a retelling of a traditional Arabic tale, a poor merchant's daughter, disguised as a boy, makes a fortune and takes revenge against seven male cousins.   PA EA F L

Siddhartha, Hermann Hesse. 1951. Paper.

This has been a cult book for several generations of young adults. Siddhartha has a variety of experiences and pleasures until he ascends to a state of peace and mystic holiness.   LA

The Tower Room, Ad'ele Geras. 1992.

Based on Rapunzel, this is the first in a series of realistic fantasies based on classic fairy tales written by a best-selling British writer. Three girls live in their tower dorm room watching a laboratory assistant who is the only man on campus. *Watching the Roses* (1992) is based on Sleeping Beauty, and *Pictures of the Night* (1993) is loosely adapted from Snow White. Each book focuses on one of the three roommates.   EA LA F

Science Fiction

Another Heaven, Another Earth, H. M. Hoover. 1981.

Survivors of an unsuccessful attempt to colonize another planet must choose between life on that doomed planet or on mechanized, overcrowded Earth.   PA EA + L

The Bell Tree, H. M. Hoover. 1982.

Henny and her father search for an ancient civilization. This book is readable by younger adolescents, but the questions it poses are not easily answered.   PA EA L

Beyond Silence, Eleanor Cameron. 1980. Paper.

Andy goes back in time nearly one hundred years and meets Deirdre.   EA

Beyond the Dark River, Monica Hughes. 1981.

An Amish boy and an Indian girl survive a nuclear holocaust and venture into a destroyed city to seek information about medicines to save dying children (L). Also try *The Crystal Drop* (1992), which deals with the subject of the threatened ozone layer.   PA EA

Blossom Culp and the Sleep of Death, Richard Peck. 1986. Paper.

Blossom is haunted by an ancient Egyptian princess. With the help of a friend, Blossom restores the princess to her rightful place in history. Other books in the Blossom series are *The Ghost Belonged to Me* (1985; paper +), *Ghosts I Have Been*

(1977; paper +); and *The Dreadful Future of Blossom Culp* (1983; paper +).   PA EA *

Brave New World, Aldous Huxley. 1932. Paper.

This is a classic story of a dehumanized future world.   LA

Deadeye Dick, Kurt Vonnegut. 1982. Paper.

Vonnegut offers his usual crop of madcap characters and humor mixed with the themes of inhumanity and technology gone wild. Older adolescents who enjoy this book may also enjoy Vonnegut's many other books.   LA

Devil on My Back, Monica Hughes. 1985.

Personal computers are attached directly to people's brains.   EA

Dune, Frank Herbert. 1965. Paper.

This space fantasy takes place on a desert planet. Mathematics whizzes are particularly fond of Herbert's books.   LA

The Dying Sun, Gary Blackwood. 1987.

This science fiction novel focuses on the contemporary concern of what will happen if the polar ice caps melt.   EA

Foundation, Isaac Asimov. 1951. Paper.

This is first of a series in which Hari Seldon creates the Foundations to preserve human culture during the dark ages after the collapse of the first galactic empire. The other books in the trilogy are *Foundation and Empire* (1983; paper) and *The Second Foundation* (1983; paper).   LA

House of Stairs, William Sleator. 1974. Paper.

Five young people are taken from state institutions to a place without walls, ceiling, or floor, but with endless stairs, to be a part of a psychological experiment on conditioned human response.   EA * +

Interstellar Pig, William Sleator. 1984. Paper.

Barney's neighbors invite him to play a game in which competing aliens do extreme things to get a smiling pink pig. Other fun-to-read science fiction books by Sleator include *The Boy Who Reversed Himself* (1986; paper), *The Duplicate* (1988; paper), *Singularity* (1985; paper), *The Spirit House* (1991), and *Strange Attractors* (1990; paper). EA * +

Keeper of the Isis Light, Monica Hughes. 1981.

Olwen does not know how different she is from others on Isis until Earth settlers arrive and she falls in love (L). Other popular science fiction books by Hughes include *Crisis on Cornshelf Ten* (1975; L) and *Invitation to the Game* (1990; paper). EA

The Martian Chronicles, Ray Bradbury. 1946. Paper.

In this series of short tales, Earthlings gain and lose Mars. EA LA

Short Stories

Baseball in April and Other Stories, Gary Soto. 1990.

This delightful collection of sports stories is sure to please the most reluctant male reader. EA * +

Break of Dark, Robert Westall. 1982.

The macabre stories here are about such things as a supernatural nude, a German pilot who keeps coming back to life, and a horse trough involved in purse snatching. EA LA L

Coming-and-Going Men: Four Tales, Paul Fleischman. 1985.

In these stories a traveling man comes in contact with the little town of New Canaan, Vermont, in 1900. LA

Early Sorrow: Ten Stories of Youth, edited by Charlotte Zolotow. 1986.

Each story here deals with a deeply traumatic moment in an adolescent's life. EA LA

Eight Plus One, Robert Cormier. 1980. Paper.

Each story is introduced with the author's thoughts about how and why it was created, making this a great tool for budding writers. EA LA +

Ghostly Tales of Love & Revenge, edited by Daniel Cohen. 1992.
This book will appeal to readers because of the chill factor. After they are hooked they will learn about other cultures since the stories come from such places as Japan, Spain, and Scotland. EA

Giving Birth to Thunder, Sleeping with His Daughter, Barry Lopez. 1978. Paper.
This is a collection of sixty-eight stories from the oral traditions of more than forty Indian tribes. EA LA +

Imaginary Lands, edited by Robin McKinley. 1986.
The setting is the most important part of each story in this volume. PA EA +

In Camera and Other Stories, Robert Westall. 1992.
These five supernatural tales are fun and easy to read and will appeal to many young readers. EA LA +

Merlyn's Pen, edited by James Stahl.
This is an unusual listing because it is not a book; it is a magazine of writing by adolescents for adolescents. Teens will find many short stories to love in each issue of this delightful publication. PA EA LA *

Sixteen: Short Stories by Outstanding Writers for Young Adults, edited by Donald R. Gallo. 1984. Paper.
All of the stories have memorable teenage characters. Also try *Center Stage: One-Act Plays for Teenage Readers and Actors* (1990; paper), *Connections* (1989; paper), and *Visions: Nineteen Short Stories by Outstanding Writers for Young Adults* (1987; paper). EA +

Summer Girls, Love Boys & Other Short Stories, Norma Fox Mazer. 1982. Paper.
These are stories about relationships that are not always what they seem. EA F *

A Touch of Chill, Joan Aiken. 1980.

These stories will keep young readers on the edge of their seats.
This is a good choice for reluctant readers.   PA EA +

A Whisper in the Night: Tales of Terror and Suspense, Joan Aiken.
1984. Paper.
This collection of suspense tales will intrigue most young readers.   PA EA +

12

Nonfiction Kids Love

Many teens, particularly boys, prefer nonfiction to fiction. Since school experience with nonfiction usually is limited to textbooks and reference books, many students are not exposed to nonfiction books written specifically for them.

The amount of nonfiction for adolescents increases each year. This annotated bibliography is organized into sections to help you select books. For an explanation of the bibliographic information that appears with each entry, see chapter 11, p. 144.

Animals

Born Free: A Lioness of Two Worlds, Joy Adamson. 1974. Paper.
    This classic, moving story of the lioness Elsa is narrated by a woman who loved her.   EA LA +
Dance of the Wolves, Roger Peters. 1985. Paper.
    A young researcher spends three winters studying the wolves of northern Michigan in this personal story.   PA EA LA
Incident at Hawk's Hill, Allan Eckert. 1971. Paper.
    In this delightful story, a six-year-old boy is cared for by a badger.   EA LA * +

Max, the Dog Who Refused to Die, Kyra Petrovskaya Wayne. 1979. Paper.

Max, a doberman, is separated from his family in Yosemite and seriously injured.   PA * +

Ourselves and Other Animals, Peter Evans. 1987.

This fascinating book deals with the interconnections between animals and humans and is based on the television series of the same name.   EA LA L

Secret Go the Wolves, R. D. Lawrence. 1980. Paper.

The author tells how he raised two wolf cubs to maturity. EA LA

The Zoo That Never Was: The Reluctant Zoo Keeper, R. D. Lawrence. 1981. Paper.

The author and his wife face resistance from local governments when they try to care for injured and helpless animals.   EA LA

. . . . . .

The Arts

Black Music in America: A History through Its People, James Haskins. 1987.

The author of *Black Theater in America* (1982; paper) discusses the development of black music from the time of slavery to the 1980s. Other excellent books by Haskins include *Black Dance in America: A History through Its People* (1990; paper) and *The Story of Stevie Wonder* (1976; L).   EA LA

Castle, David Macaulay. 1982. Paper.

Macaulay's wonderful, artistic books are difficult to categorize. This one presents pen-and-ink drawings of a castle. Other excellent pen-and-ink books by this author/illustrator include *Cathedral: The Story of Its Construction* (1981; paper), *City: A Story of Roman Planning and Construction* (1983), *Great Moments in*

Architecture (1978), *Pyramid* (1982; paper), and *The Way Things Work* (1988; paper).   PA EA LA

Chapters: My Growth as a Writer, Lois Duncan. 1982.

This autobiography of a popular writer of books for young adults appeals to adolescents who hope to have a career in writing.   EA LA F

The Cookcamp, Gary Paulsen. 1991. Paper. *Woodsong*. 1990. Paper.

These memoirs are particularly appropriate for adolescents who have enjoyed the exciting fictional adventure books of this gifted storyteller.   PA EA

Duke Ellington, James Lincoln Collier. 1987. Paper.

This followup to *Louis Armstrong: An American Genius* (1983) deals mainly with Ellington's band and music.   EA LA

A Girl from Yamhill: A Memoir, Beverly Cleary. 1988. Paper.

This is an autobiographical account of well-known children's writer Beverly Cleary's young life. Cleary fans will enjoy reading about the events of her life that helped her become a popular author.   PA EA

I Have Words to Spend: Reflections of a Small-Town Editor, Robert Cormier. 1991. Paper.

Robert Cormier is one of the most highly regarded authors of fiction for young adults. In this memoir he discusses his life as a newspaper editor and how it relates to his fiction.   EA LA

Nothing but the Best: The Struggle for Perfection at the Juilliard School, Judith Kogan. 1987. Paper.

The story of America's most prestigious school for the arts is told from the perspective of former students.   EA LA

Nothing but the Blues, edited by Lawrence Cohn. 1993.

This is a comprehensive, well-illustrated history of blues music for blues fans.   EA LA

The Pigman & Me, Paul Zindel. 1992. Paper.

This is an autobiographical account of a gifted young adult

writer who in spite of his difficult youth—or, perhaps, because of it—became a writer. EA

The Place My Words Are Looking For: What Poets Say About and Through Their Work, edited by Paul B. Janeczko. 1990.

Teacher and poet Janeczko has compiled this wonderful book about poetry and poets. Another excellent book for the budding poet is Janeczko's *Poetspeak: In Their Work, About Their Work* (1983; paper). EA LA

Presenting Robert Cormier, Patricia J. Campbell. 1985. Paper.

This first biography in the Twayne U.S. Young Adult Authors' series deals not only with Cormier's life but also examines his books and his writing style. Each biography in the series is excellent for adolescents interested in a particular author, his or her books, or in writing; other books in the series include *Presenting Judy Blume* (Maryann N. Weidt, 1991; paper), *Presenting Sue Ellen Bridgers* (Ted Hipple, 1990), *Presenting Rosa Guy* (Jerrie Norris, 1988; paper), *Presenting S. E. Hinton* (Jay Daly, 1989; paper), *Presenting M. E. Kerr* (Alleen P. Nilsen, 1986; paper), *Presenting Madeleine L'Engle* (Donald R. Hettinga, 1993), *Presenting Norma Fox Mazer* (Sally H. Holtze, 1989; paper), and *Presenting Richard Peck* (Donald Gallo, 1989; paper). EA LA

Reaching for Dreams: A Ballet from Rehearsal to Opening Night, Susan Kuklin. 1987.

A beautifully photographed, vivid depiction of the ballet that appeals to younger adolescents who dream of a career in dance. PA EA *

Speaking for Ourselves, Too: More Autobiographical Sketches by Notable Authors of Books for Young Adults, edited by Donald R. Gallo. 1993.

This second volume presents authors writing about how they became authors. The book is fun to read and encouraging to would-be writers. PA EA LA

To All Gentleness: William Carlos Williams, The Doctor Poet, Neil Baldwin. 1984.

A beautifully told biography of a remarkable man who combined his love of medicine with his love for poetry. EA LA + L

Uncommon Eloquence: A Biography of Angna Enters, Dorothy Mandel. 1986.

Angna Enters was a gifted writer, dancer/mime, set designer, and artist from the 1920s through the 1970s. This story may inspire older adolescent girls. LA F

Winter Season: A Dancer's Journal, Toni Bently. 1982. Paper.

This story of the New York City Ballet's winter season of 1980–81 is told from the perspective of one of its ballerinas. EA LA F

. . . . . .

Biography and Autobiography

Alicia: My Story, Alicia Appleman-Jurman. 1990. Paper.

This is an autobiography of a Jewish girl who was able to escape imprisonment in a Nazi concentration camp. EA LA

American Dreams: Lost and Found, Studs Terkel. 1980. Paper.

Mini-biographies of the great, the near great, and the not-so-great are recounted by one of America's foremost oral anthropologists. LA

Anne Frank, The Diary of a Young Girl, Anne Frank. 1946. Paper.

This is the day-by-day account of a young Jewish girl forced to hide in an attic from June 1942 to August 1944. Readers fascinated by Anne Frank's short life will also enjoy *The Last Seven Months of Anne Frank* by Willy Lindwer (1991; paper) and *Anne Frank—Beyond the Diary: A Photographic Remembrance* (Ruud Van der Rol and Rian Verhoeven, 1993). PA EA

Beyond the Myth: The Story of Joan of Arc, Polly Schoyer Brooks. 1990.

This fictionalized biography of Joan, who was burned at the stake at nineteen, presents her as a normal, healthy peasant girl who possesses both shrewdness and idealism. PA EA +

Blue Hills Remembered: A Recollection, Rosemary Sutcliff. 1984.

The author traces her beginnings from a lonely child of a British naval officer to a gifted writer of historical fiction. EA LA F + L

Boston Boy, Nat Hentoff. 1986.

Writer Nat Hentoff explores the impact on his writing of his years in Boston, from early childhood to early adulthood. LA L

The First Woman Doctor, Rachel Baker. 1987. Paper.

This is an easy-to-read biography of Elizabeth Blackwell, who practiced medicine in the nineteenth century. PA *

Grace in the Wilderness: After the Liberation, Aranka Siegal. 1985. Paper.

This sequel to *Upon the Head of the Goat* (1981; paper) is the story of Piri Davidowitz's life after she was liberated from Auschwitz. Since it covers her adolescent years, it is of particular interest to teens. EA LA

Hold On to Love, Mollie Hunter. 1984.

This wonderful sequel to *A Sound of Chariots* (1972; paper) reads more like a novel than an autobiography of the life of this well-known British author. EA LA * + L

The Horns of the Moon: A Short Biography of Adolf Hitler, Gene Smith. 1973.

This book deals with Hitler's first love, his boyhood friends, and his fascination with astrology, and relates these experiences to what he later becomes. PA EA L

I Am Fifteen—and I Don't Want to Die, Christine Arnothy. 1950. Paper.

This is an autobiographical account of a young woman who survived the Hungarian Holocaust.   EA LA +

I Know Why the Caged Bird Sings, Maya Angelou. 1970. Paper.
This first volume in the autobiography of a gifted African American singer, dancer, and poet is particularly appropriate for adolescents because it recounts Angelou's childhood and early adolescence. Some parts are disturbing and graphic.   LA F

Isaac Bashevis Singer: The Story of a Storyteller, Paul Kresh. 1984.
This biography traces Singer's life from his childhood in Poland to his 1978 Nobel Prize for literature.   PA EA

Lincoln: A Photobiography, Russell Freedman. 1987. Paper.
This book, by a gifted writer, not only provides excellent, rarely seen pictures of Lincoln, but also a first-rate account of his life.   PA EA

Malcolm X: By Any Means Necessary, Walter Dean Myers. 1993. Paper.
This excellent, revealing account of the life of Malcolm X is particularly appropriate for young readers.   PA EA

The Right Stuff, Tom Wolfe. 1979. Paper.
This is the story of the early NASA test pilots.   EA LA

Sojourner Truth: Ain't I a Woman?, Patricia C. McKissack and Frederick McKissack. 1992.
This award-winning team has produced another easy-to-read, well-researched historical and biographical account in the fascinating life of a slave who escapes and wins a court case to free her son.   PA EA * +

· · · · · ·
Careers

American Almanac of Jobs and Salaries, John Wright. Paper.
This frequently updated work provides information on numerous career and job opportunities.   EA LA

Callback, Ginger Howard Friedman. Paper.

This is an excellent book for adolescents interested in an acting career.   EA LA

Careers series. Paper.

Young adults exploring career options are likely to be interested in the following books in this series: *Careers for Women as Clergy* (Julie F. Parker, 1993), *Careers as an Animal Rights Activist* (Shelly Field, 1993), *Careers as a Rock Musician* (Del Hopkins and Margaret Hopkins, 1993), *Careers for Women in Politics* (Richard S. Lee and Mary Price Lee, 1993), *Careers as a Flight Attendant* (Catherine O. Lobus, 1991), *Careers as an Electrician* (Elizabeth S. Lytle, 1993), and *Careers in Firefighting* (Mary Price Lee and Richard S. Lee, 1993).   PA EA *

The Children of Santa Clara, Elizabeth Marek. 1987.

A young woman discovers herself through her work with special children in this sensitive story.   EA LA *

Fashion Drawing: The Basic Principles, Anne Allen and Julian Seaman. 1993. Paper.

This is a fascinating primer for young adults interested in a career in fashion design.   EA LA

I Am a Teacher: A Tribute to America's Teachers, compiled by David Marshall Marquis and Robin Sachs. 1990. Paper.

This excellent book makes it clear that in spite of criticism there are many marvelous teachers in U.S. schools. Although this book is written primarily for adults, young adults thinking about a career in education are likely to find it inspirational.   LA

Small Victories: The Real World of a Teacher, Her Students, and Their High School, Samuel G. Freedman. 1990. Paper.

The author spent a year shadowing Jessica Sigel at Seward Park High School in Manhattan.   EA LA

Working, Studs Terkel. 1974. Paper.

This is the premier oral history of working people in America.   EA LA

. . . . . .
Multicultural

Anthony Burns: The Defeat and Triumph of a Fugitive Slave, Virginia Hamilton. 1988.
This is an excellent account about ten days in the life of Anthony Burns, who attempted to escape from slavery in Virginia and whose plight galvanized the abolitionists in Boston in 1854.   PA EA

Black Americans: A History in Their Own Words, edited by Milton Meltzer. 1984. Paper.
Meltzer uses the writings of hundreds of African Americans to help young readers understand the black experience in America.   PA EA LA

Black Like Me, John Howard Griffin. 1977. Paper.
A white man disguises himself as a black and travels through the Deep South in this classic story.   LA

The Chinese of America, Jack Chen. 1982.
The role of the Chinese in American history is examined in this comprehensive historical and social account appropriate for mature readers.   LA L

Farewell to Manzanar, Jeanne Wakatsuki Houston and James Houston. 1973. Paper.
A young Japanese girl's life in a relocation camp during World War II is depicted in this moving story.   EA LA *

Freedom Train: The Story of Harriet Tubman, Dorothy Sterling. 1987. Paper.
This book presents the story of Tubman, who risked her life to help others escape to freedom.   PA EA *

Growing Up Native American, edited by Patricia Riley. 1993.
The work of twenty-two writers from fifteen nations across the United States and Canada is gathered in this anthology.   MA LA

Indian Chiefs, Russell Freedman. 1987. Paper.

This is a beautifully illustrated, well-documented narrative of six Indian chiefs, including Red Cloud and Sitting Bull. PA EA LA *

An Indian Winter, Russell Freedman. 1992.

This book by a well-known young adult author and historian is about the Mandan Indians of North Dakota. EA

Manchild in the Promised Land, Claude Brown. 1965. Paper.

This is a memoir of childhood in Harlem by a man who pulled himself up from drugs, crime, and poverty. LA

Many Thousand Gone: African Americans from Slavery to Freedom, Virginia Hamilton. 1993.

This book provides many individual profiles of slaves, including Harriet Tubman and Frederick Douglass, and is written in Hamilton's interesting, lively style. PA EA LA +

Mississippi Challenge, Mildred Pitts Walter. 1992.

This book traces the political history of African Americans from the Civil War through the late 1960s. EA LA

Narrative of the Life of Frederick Douglass an American Slave: Written by Himself, Frederick Douglass. 1845. Paper.

In this classic slave narrative, Frederick Douglass talks of the young years before his freedom. He gives a most moving account of the importance of education to our freedom. LA +

New Kids on the Block: Oral Histories of Immigrant Teens, Janet Bode. 1989.

Young immigrants from recent decades talk about what it is like to be different and want to be included. EA *

Now Is Your Time! The African-American Struggle for Freedom, Walter Dean Myers. 1992.

This is an excellent, readable history of African Americans by a gifted writer of young adult books. PA EA

Paul Robeson: The Life and Times of a Free Black Man, Virginia Hamilton. 1974.

Fewer than 250 pages, this is a well-researched account of the singer's life, including the disruption of his career in the United States because of his political sympathy for the Soviet Union.   PA EA

Roots, Alex Haley. 1976. Paper.

This fictionalized history presents a seven-generation story of a family from its roots in West Africa to the plantations of pre–Civil War America.   EA LA +

To Be a Slave, Julius Lester. 1968. Paper.

The narrative graphically describes the experiences of men and women who lived as slaves. Lester has also edited two excellent anthologies of black folktales for young adults: *Black Folktales* (1969) and *Long Journey Home: Stories from Black History and Folktales* (1972; paper).   LA

· · · · · ·

Handicaps and Illness

AIDS: The Ultimate Challenge, Elizabeth Kübler-Ross. 1987.

This is a frank discussion with friends, families, and AIDS victims.   EA LA

Brian's Song, William Blinn. Paper.

The book tells of football star Brian Piccolo's life and career, which was cut short by cancer.   EA LA *

Death Be Not Proud: A Memoir, John Gunther. 1949. Paper.

This much loved book was written as a tribute to the author's adolescent son who died of cancer.   EA LA +

If We Could Hear the Grass Grow, Eleanor Craig. 1983.

The author recounts her experiences with severely disturbed children during a summer at Camp Hopewell.   EA LA

One Child, Torey L. Hayden. 1980. Paper.

A story of emotionally disturbed children is told with insight and compassion by their teacher.   EA LA

Questions and Answers on AIDS, Lyn Frumkin and John Leonard. 1993. Paper.

Unbiased answers to nearly two hundred questions dealing with all aspects of AIDS are frankly presented.   EA LA

Robyn's Book: A True Diary, Robyn Miller. 1990. Paper.

Robyn, who died of cystic fibrosis at the age of twenty-one, tells her own story.   PA EA LA F

The Story of My Life, Helen Keller. 1954. Paper.

This is the remarkable story of a woman who overcame deafness and blindness.   PA EA LA +

. . . . . .

History and Government

The American Promise: Voices of a Changing Nation, 1945–Present, edited by Milton Meltzer. 1990.

The book deals with developments since World War II: the atomic bomb, the Cold War, Korea, Vietnam, the civil rights movement, the generation gap, the women's movement, immigration, poverty, and chemical pollution.   EA LA

The American Revolutionaries: A History in Their Own Words, 1750–1800, edited by Milton Meltzer. 1987.

A fascinating account of the Revolution told by the people who experienced it is provided by the gifted editor/writer. PA EA LA +

The Americans I: The Colonial Experience, 1958; *The Americans II: The National Experience*, 1975; *The Americans III: The Democratic Experience*, 1973. Daniel J. Boorstin. Paper.

These books have won numerous prizes for their accurate and readable portrayal of American history.   LA

Anarchism: Political Innocence or Social Violence?, James Forman. 1975.

This book is one of a series of excellent books by historian

Forman on various forms of government (L). Other recommended books in the series include *Capitalism: Economic Individualism to Today's Welfare State* (1972; L), *Communism: From Marx's Manifesto to Twentieth Century Reality* (1972; L), *Fascism: The Meaning and Experience of Reactionary Revolutions* (1974), *Nazism* (1978; L), and *Socialism: Its Theoretical Roots and Present-Day Development* (1972). EA

Brother, Can You Spare a Dime? The Great Depression, 1929–1933, Milton Meltzer. 1977.

Firsthand accounts woven into the history of the Depression make this book fascinating. EA

Columbus and the World around Him, Milton Meltzer. 1990.

Like all of Meltzer's books, *Columbus* brings to life the historical figure, his life, and his times. PA EA

Decision in Philadelphia: The Constitutional Convention of 1787, James Lincoln Collier and Christopher Collier. 1986. Paper.

This is an interesting and easy-to-read account of one of the most important events in the early days of the U.S. government. PA EA

The Eagle and the Dragon: The History of U.S.—China Relations, Don Lawson. 1985.

The author traces the two-hundred-year history of America's relationship with China. EA LA

Eyes on the Prize: America's Civil Rights Years, 1954–1965, Juan Williams. 1987. Paper.

This companion volume to the PBS television series that chronicles the civil rights movement is fascinating reading. EA LA +

Gentle Annie: The True Story of a Civil War Nurse, Mary Francis Shura. 1991.

This is an excellent book for readers who are fascinated by real people who lived during important historical events. PA EA

If I Die in a Combat Zone, Tim O'Brien. 1973. Paper.

This is a powerful, graphic book about one soldier's experiences in Vietnam. LA

The Jews: Story of a People, Howard Fast. 1982. Paper.

This wonderfully illustrated and photographed account traces the four-thousand-year history of the Jewish people. EA LA

Lines of Battle, Annette Tapert. 1987.

A series of letters written by World War II GIs helps bring the horrors of war to life. EA LA

The Mad Game, James Forman. 1980.

Examining the question of why we have war, Forman traces the history of war from the beginnings of human history to the Russian invasion of Afghanistan. He looks at peacemaking efforts that have been made as well as at ways to stop us from destroying the earth. EA LA L

Never to Forget: The Jews of the Holocaust, Milton Meltzer. 1976. Paper.

This is a carefully researched and compassionate account of the real people of the Holocaust. PA EA LA * +

The Pantheon Documentary Comic Books Series. Includes *Trotsky for Beginners*, Tariq Ali (1980; paper); *Freud for Beginners*, Richard Appignanesi and Oscar Zarate (1979; paper); *Lenin for Beginners*, Richard Appignanesi (1979); *Economics for Beginners*, Bernard Caravan (1982; L); *Ecology for Beginners*, Stephen Croall (1981); *Capitalism for Beginners*, Robert Lekachman (1981; paper); *Einstein for Beginners*, Michael McGuinness and Joe Schwartz (1979; paper); *Darwin for Beginners*, Jonathan Miller (1982; paper); *Mao for Beginners*, Rius (1980); *Marx for Beginners*, Rius (1980; paper) and *Marx's Kapital for Beginners*, David Smith (1982; L). This clever series unites illustrations with humorous text about highly sophisticated subjects. Because several are unfortunately out of print, libraries are the best source. PA *

Scalded to Death by Steam, Katie Letcher Lyle. 1983. Paper.
This unusual book is about little-known railroad disasters and the ballads written about them.   EA LA

Ten Days That Shook the World, John Reed. 1960. Paper.
This is a first-person account of the ten days that followed the Bolshevik takeover of Russia.   EA LA

They Had a Dream: The Civil Rights Struggle from Frederick Douglass to Marcus Garvey to Martin Luther King, Jr., to Malcolm X, Jules Archer. 1993.
Excellent, readable political biographies of four great American leaders are integrated into a history of the civil rights struggle.   EA LA

· · · · · ·

How-To Books

How to Study, Harry Maddox. 1983. Paper.
This book is designed to help students develop more productive study habits and more efficient thinking.   EA LA

I Hate School!: How to Hang In and When to Drop Out, Claudine G. Wirths and Mary Bowman-Kruhm. 1986. Paper.
This book for kids who are thinking of dropping out of school gives good, appropriate advice on how to survive in school, without promising success.   PA EA LA *

John Hedgecoe's Photography Basics, John Hedgecoe. 1993.
Like Hedgecoe's earlier books, this book contains helpful hints and photographic illustrations for beginning and experienced photographers.   EA LA

Learn to Draw 3-D, Doug DuBosque. 1992. Paper.
This is a great guide for budding artists who want to try something different.   PA EA LA *

Losing Someone You Love: When a Brother or Sister Dies, Elizabeth Richter. 1986.

This is a frank, helpful guide for dealing with sorrow, fear, loneliness, and anger. PA EA LA L

The Mentor Guide to Term Papers and Reports, William C. Paxson. 1988. Paper.

This student-oriented guide includes sample papers, stylistic tips, and hints for all stages of paper writing. EA LA

Safe, Strong, and Streetwise, Helen Benedict. 1986. Paper.

This is one of those books we wish adolescents did not need. It discusses the dangers of the streets and helps teens deal with them. PA EA LA

The String on a Roast Won't Catch Fire in the Oven: An A–Z Encyclopedia of Common Sense for Newly Independent Young Adults, Candice Kohl. 1993. Paper.

This is a great gift of common sense advice for adolescents who are going to college or getting their first apartment. LA *

Writing Your Own Plays: Creating, Adapting, Improvising, Carol Korty. 1986.

This is a helpful guide for budding playwrights. EA LA

Your First Job, Ron Fry. 1993. Paper.

This is an informative guide for high school graduates on how to find and keep a job. LA

· · · · · ·

Humor

All Creatures Great and Small, 1972, paper; *All Things Bright and Beautiful*, 1975, paper; *All Things Wise and Wonderful*, 1977, paper; *The Lord God Made Them All*, 1981, paper; and *Every Living Thing*, 1992; James Herriot.

These are wonderfully funny accounts of life as a Yorkshire, England, veterinarian. EA LA +

The Boat Who Wouldn't Float, Farley Mowat. 1970. Paper.

This is an adventure story about the people of Newfoundland and the sea. EA LA +

Cheaper by the Dozen, 1948, and *Belles on Their Toes*, 1950, Frank B. Gilbreth, Jr., and Ernestine Gilbreth Carey. Paper.
These delightful books about the Gilbreth family are sure to continue to keep teens laughing. PA EA * +

The Dog Who Wouldn't Be, Farley Mowat. 1957. Paper.
The story of Mowat's boyhood with Mutt is very humorous. EA LA +

Teenage Romance: Or How to Die of Embarrassment, Delia Ephron. 1981. Paper.
This book provides humorous advice for a teen experiencing her first romance. EA LA F

· · · · · ·
Math and Puzzles

Challenging Lateral Thinking Puzzles, Paul Sloan and Des Mac-Hale. 1993. Paper.
More than ninety brainteasers for teenagers are presented here. PA EA

The Complete Poems to Solve, May Swenson. 1993.
This fun collection is appropriate for young people who enjoy riddle poems and logic puzzles. The puzzles range from the obvious to the subtle and involve interesting language usage. PA EA +

Hidden Logic Puzzles, Charles Weaver. 1993. Paper.
More than 150 conundrums and cryptograms challenge teenagers to think logically and utilize mathematics skills. EA LA

World's Hardest Puzzles, Charles Barry Townsend. 1993. Paper.
This thin volume contains almost one hundred difficult logic puzzles for teenagers who enjoy mathematical challenges. EA LA

Realm of Algebra and *Realm of Numbers* (L), Isaac Asimov. Paper.
   A prolific and popular science fiction writer explains the whys
   and wherefores of algebra and mathematics. EA LA

• • • • • •
Myths, Legends, and Parascience

Ancient Myths, Norma Lorre Goodrich. 1960. Paper.
   Vivid retellings of myths of Greece, India, Egypt, Rome, Crete,
   Persia, and Sumer make this book fascinating. LA
Beowulf, adapted by Rosemary Sutcliff. 1984.
   A gifted author of young adult books retells the classic story
   of Beowulf and the monster Grendel. PA EA LA
Communion: A True Story, Whitley Strieber. 1987. Paper.
   This is a true story about an individual who experienced an
   unexplained phenomenon. EA LA
*From Sea to Shining Sea: A Treasury of American Folklore and Folk
   Songs*, edited by Amy L. Cohn. 1993.
   This delightful book presents stories and songs brought to
   America by immigrants. PA EA LA +
The Man Who Wanted Seven Wives, Katie Letcher Lyle. 1986.
   The basis for this book is a murder mystery that was suppos-
   edly solved by the testimony of a ghost. EA LA
Medieval Myths, Norma Lorre Goodrich. 1961. Paper.
   The myths collected here from Scandinavia, Wales, France,
   Austria, Russia, and Spain will interest teens. EA LA
The Sword in the Stone, T. H. White. 1938. Paper.
   This classic book chronicles the young life and adventures of
   the boy who became King Arthur. PA EA +
They Dance in the Sky: Native American Star Myths, Jean Guard
   Monroe and Ray A. Williamson. 1987.
   This collection of American Indian myths dealing with stars
   makes interesting reading. PA EA LA * + L

. . . . . .

Personal and Family Problems

Boys and Sex (3rd edition) and *Girls and Sex* (3rd edition), Wardell B. Pomeroy. 1991. Paper.
These revised editions are designed to tell boys and girls and
their parents what they need to know about growing up and
modern sex roles.   EA LA +

The Boys' and Girls' Book about Divorce (revised edition), Richard
A. Gardner. 1992. Paper.
This book is based on the author's thirteen years of therapeutic
work with divorced parents and their children.   PA

The Eight Hundred–Cocaine Book of Drugs and Alcohol Recovery,
James Cocores. 1990. Paper.
This frequently revised, complete guide to America's fastest-
growing drug problem is helpful to teens and adults.   EA LA

In Love and in Danger, Barrie Levy. 1993.
This provocative book provides a warning to girls about power
and dependency in relationships. It presents the personal accounts of two abused young women.   LA

It Won't Happen to Me: Teenagers Talk about Pregnancy, Paula
McGuire. Paper.
Fifteen adolescents talk frankly about pregnancy and mother-
hood.   PA EA LA F

Kids Having Kids: The Unwed Teenage Parent, Janet Bode. 1980.
This informative book discusses the sexual conduct of teenagers and the health risks associated with pregnancy and birth
control. Options such as adoption, abortion, and keeping the
child are frankly discussed (L). *Kids Still Having Kids: People
Talk About Teen Pregnancy* (1993) is a continuation of the discussion on the same topic. The strength of both books is
Bode's interviews with teenagers.   EA LA F *

Let's Eat Right to Keep Fit (1983) and *Let's Stay Healthy: A Guide to Lifelong Nutrition* (1983) Adelle Davis (edited and expanded by Ann Gildroy). Paper.

These are popular guides for eating well and staying healthy. EA LA

Loving Each Other, 1984; *Living, Loving, and Learning*, 1982; and *Love*, 1972; Leo Buscaglia. Paper.

These sensitive, thought-provoking books deal with love, life, and relationships. PA EA LA

Sex, Drugs, and AIDS, Oralee Wachter. 1987. Paper.

Based on a highly acclaimed film, this book answers crucial questions for teens and their parents. PA EA LA

Sexual Harassment, Elaine Landau. 1993.

The author defines sexual harassment in terms of power and its abuse. She discusses specific cases, the lack of definition in the courts, as well as the importance of the Anita Hill testimony. EA LA

Straight Talk about Student Life, Christine Dentenmaro and Rachel Kranz. 1993.

This book, dealing with school-related problems, is a part of the "Straight Talk" series. It provides advice on coping with school and social pressures. PA EA

Unspeakable Acts: The Ordeal of Thomas Waters-Rimmer, Greggory W. Morris and Thomas J. Waters-Rimmer. 1993.

Waters-Rimmer examines his childhood in which he was physically abused by his natural father and sexually abused by a foster father. The book can give help and encouragement to abused teens. EA LA

Where Are My Birth Parents? A Guide for Teenage Adoptees, Karen Gravelle and Susan Fischer. 1993.

The authors make a case and give suggestions for adoptees who wish to pursue their heritage. EA LA

· · · · · ·

Poetry

Back to Class, Mel Glenn. 1988.

This is one anthology of poems by a teacher-poet about his students, their school, and their teachers.   PA EA

Black Hair, Gary Soto. 1985.

This is an excellent anthology of family poems by a well-known Chicano poet.   EA LA + L

The Break Dance Kids: Poems of Sport, Motion, and Locomotion, 1985; *The Sidewalk Racer and Other Poems of Sports and Motion*, 1977 (L); Lillian Morrison.

Morrison is a master at catching motion and sports in poetry.   PA EA LA * +

Bring Me All Your Dreams, edited by Nancy Larrick. 1988. Paper.

Fifty-six dream poems have been collected by this poet and educator.   PA EA LA * +

Class Dismissed! High School Poems, 1982, and *Class Dismissed Two: More High School Poems*, 1986, Mel Glenn. Paper.

Glenn's poems catch the essence of the school experience.   PA EA * +

Don't Forget to Fly, edited by Paul Janeczko. 1981.

Janeczko has collected modern poems that reflect a range of human emotions (L). Other works by Janeczko include *Going Over to Your Place: Poems for Each Other* (1987); *Pocket Poems: Selected for a Journey* (1985); *Postcard Poems: A Collection of Poems for Sharing* (1979; L); and *Strings: A Gathering of Family Poems* (1984).   PA EA LA *

I Am Phoenix: Poems for Two Voices, Paul Fleischman. 1985. Paper.

All the poems included here are written to be read aloud by two readers at once.   EA LA

If I Were in Charge of the World and Other Worries, Judith Viorst. 1981. Paper.
> This delightful collection of poetry about the preadolescent experience is sure to amuse.   PA * +

A Latch Against the Wind, Victoria Forrester. 1985.
> These poems about emotions, poetry, dawn, seasons, fairies, and nature are appropriate for older adolescents.   LA L

Love Is Like the Lion's Tooth: An Anthology of Love Poems, compiled by Frances McCullough. 1984.
> The poems in this collection deal with the effects and stages of love.   EA LA

Love Lines: Poetry in Person, Betsy Hearne. 1987.
> These love poems are sure to be enjoyed by adolescents.   PA EA LA *

Monkey Puzzle and Other Poems, Myra Cohn Livingston. 1984.
> This book contains short poems about trees for children and adolescents. Also try *A Time to Talk: Poems of Friendship* (1992).   EA LA +

My Friend's Got This Problem, Mr. Chandler, Mel Glenn. 1991.
> Many of these poems highlight the teaching profession while others talk about adolescents and their problems.   EA LA * +

O Frabjous Day: Poetry for Holidays and Celebrations, collected by Myra Cohn Livingston. 1977.
> This is a wonderful collection of poems to help celebrate nearly every holiday.   PA EA LA * + L

Rainbows Are Made: Poems by Carl Sandburg, collected by Lee Bennett Hopkins. 1984.
> This short anthology makes Sandburg's poetry accessible to all readers. Other collections by Hopkins include *My Mane Catches the Wind: Poems about Horses* (1979; L), *Munching: Poems about Eating* (1985), and *A Song in Stone: City Poems* (1983; L).   PA EA LA * +

Saturday's Children: Poems of Work, edited by Helen Plotz. 1982.
These poems deal with the emotions of work.   LA + L

Those Who Ride the Night Winds, Nikki Giovanni. 1983. Paper.
Warm, upbeat poems discuss the black experience through the
eyes of a gifted African American poet.   LA +

Why Am I Grown So Cold? Poems of the Unknowable, edited by
Myra Cohn Livingston. 1982.
Poems dealing with the supernatural are interesting to
teens.   EA LA

· · · · · ·

Science and Nature

Arctic Dreams: Imagination and Desire in a Northern Landscape,
Barry Lopez. 1986. Paper.
This is a beautiful, imaginative book on the power of nature
and imagination.   LA

Cosmos, Carl Sagan. 1980. Paper.
This extraordinary book about the galaxy is based on a PBS
television series.   EA LA

Habitats: Saving Wild Places, Dorothy Hinshaw Patent. 1993.
This book focuses on how the United States has attempted to
preserve, restore, and create wildlife habitats. The author suggests ways young readers can attract wildlife to their back-
yards.   PA EA

The Lives of a Cell: Notes of a Biology Watcher, Lewis Thomas.
1974. Paper.
This biology book makes science accessible to all readers.
LA +

The Medusa and the Snail: More Notes of a Biology Watcher, Lewis
Thomas. 1979. Paper.
Another well-written, fascinating book by biologist Thomas is
must reading for budding scientists.   LA +

Modern Sports Science, Larry Kettelkamp. 1986.

This is an informative book for student athletes as well as students interested in sports science as a career.   PA EA LA

On the Loose, Terry Russell and Renny Russell. 1979. Paper.

This beautiful book about nature examines our responsibility to preserve it.   EA LA +

A Passion to Know: 20 Profiles in Science, edited by Allen L. Hammond. 1984.

Diverse scientists are discussed in this carefully edited work. A perfect book for students who are considering careers in science.   PA EA LA L

The Riddle of the Dinosaur, John Noble Wilford. 1985. Paper.

A Pulitzer prize–winning science writer attempts to solve the riddle of the dinosaur in this thought-provoking book.   EA LA

A Whale for the Killing, Farley Mowat. 1972. Paper.

This is a true account of Mowat's attempt to save a rare fin whale.   EA LA +

Whale Watch, Ada Graham and Frank Graham. 1978. Paper.

This is an interesting account of whaling and whales.   PA EA *

Wildlife of the Rainforest, Andrew Mitchell. 1989.

An excellent account of life in this unusual and threatened ecosystem is provided.   EA L

A Young Person's Guide to Science: Ideas that Change the World, Roy A. Gallant. 1993.

The organization of this book is based on the theme of humanity: humans and other species, humans and the environment, the origin of humans, and how humans imperil the earth.   EA

The Youngest Science: Notes of a Medicine Watcher, Lewis Thomas. 1983. Paper.

Thomas looks back on his own experiences as a medical student.   PA EA LA +

. . . . . .

Social Issues

AIDS: In Search of a Killer, Suzanne Levert. 1987.

   This book provides basic information on the virus and two
   moving accounts of AIDS victims.   LA

The Bill of Rights: How We Got It and What It Means, Milton
   Meltzer. 1990.

   Meltzer not only examines the history of the Bill of Rights, but
   provides a commentary on its application today.   EA LA

Discrimination, Angela Phillips. 1993.

   This book, part of the "Past and Present" series, features short
   sketches of global and historical discrimination. Although none
   of the cases is presented in depth, each provide interesting
   comparative information for adolescents.   PA EA

An Evil Cradling, Brian Keenan. 1993.

   This book chronicles the author's captivity by Shi'ite Muslims
   and his friendship with fellow hostage John McCarthy.   LA

*The First Freedom: The Tumultuous History of Free Speech in Amer-
   ica*, Nat Hentoff. 1979. Paper.

   Though now a bit dated, this book still gives one of the best
   historical accounts of the First Amendment right of free speech.
   Other excellent books by Hentoff include *The Day They Came
   to Arrest the Book* (1982; paper) and *Does This School Have
   Capital Punishment?* (1981; paper).   EA LA

The Morning After: Fear, Sex, and Feminism on College Campuses,
   Katie Roiphe. 1993.

   This mature, controversial book examines the issue of date
   rape, particularly on college campuses.   LA

*Out of the Shadows of Night: The Struggle for International Human
   Rights*, Marvin E. Frankel and Ellen Saideman. 1989.

   The struggle for international human rights and U.S. involvement in it is chronicled here.   EA LA

Poverty in America, Milton Meltzer. 1986.

Meltzer gives a lucid account of reasons for poverty and people who experience it.   EA LA

Somebody Else's Kids, Torey L. Hayden. 1981. Paper.

These stories of children rejected by much of society are told here by their teacher.   EA LA

South African Dispatches: Letters to My Countrymen, Donald Wood. 1987.

The selections in this book were originally columns in the *Daily Dispatch* published prior to Wood's arrest in 1977. They give a picture of South Africa's people and politics.   LA

Speaking Out: Teenagers Take on Race, Sex and Identity, Susan Kuklin. 1993.

Teenagers in a New York City high school discuss the difficult issues that face them. The book is direct and honest and most appropriate for mature readers and discussion with parents. EA LA

Talking Peace: A Vision for the Next Generation, Jimmy Carter. 1992.

Former president Carter discusses peace negotiations and conflict resolution in language that can easily be understood by young readers.   PA EA +

Voices from the Future: Children Speak about Violence in America, edited by Susan Goodwillie. 1993.

This book contains interviews of teenagers by teenaged reporters. The recurring theme in the interviews is violence. EA LA *

Voices of South Africa: Growing Up in a Troubled Land, Carolyn Meyer. 1986.

These powerful personal accounts of South Africa are told by young people who live there.   PA EA LA

When and Where I Enter: The Impact of Black Women on Race and Sex in America, Paula Giddings. 1984. Paper.

This is a fascinating analytical history of black women activists. LA

• • • • • •

Sports

Amazing but True Sports Stories, Phyllis Hollander and Zander Hollander. 1986. Paper.
Eighty fascinating sports stories that will delight all ages. PA EA LA

Baseball, Oxmon, 1993.
This book contains forty years of baseball stories from *Sports Illustrated*. EA LA

Champions: Stories of Ten Remarkable Athletes, Bill Litchfield, 1993.
Male and female athletes from nine sports are profiled in this book. EA

GO! FIGHT! WIN! The NCAA Guide for Cheerleaders, Betty Lou Phillips. 1981. Paper.
This book for cheerleaders and would-be cheerleaders gives advice on how to make the squad and how to become a champion squad. PA EA LA

The Illustrated Sports Record Book, Zander Hollander and David Schulz. 1991. Paper.
This is a book of records for sports enthusiasts. PA EA LA *

The Legend of Dr. J: The Story of Julius Erving, Marty Bell. 1976. Paper.
This biography of a great basketball player will be enjoyed by fans. EA LA *

Oh, Baby, I Love It!, Tim McCarver and Ray Robinson. 1987. Paper.
Sportscaster Tim McCarver talks about professional baseball from his perspective. EA LA M

Soccer Techniques, Tactics & Teamwork, Gerhard Bauer. 1993. Paper.

Great color photographs and numerous diagrams and charts make this a very enjoyable and useful book for soccer players and fans. PA EA LA *

Take It to the Mat, Bobby Douglas. 1993. Paper.

Black and white photographs illustrate this how-to book on wrestling. PA EA LA *

The Truly Great: The Two Hundred Best Football Players of All Time, Rich Korch. 1993. Paper.

Through interviews of more than three hundred players, sport writers, and coaches, Korch provides profiles of the "best" professional football players, active or retired, at all positions. EA LA *

"You Are the Coach" series, including *Baseball: It's Your Team, You Are the Coach: Basketball, You Are the Coach: College Football, You Are the Coach: College Basketball* (L), *You Are the Coach: Football, Hockey: You Are the Coach, You Are the Manager: Baseball*, Nate Aaseng. Paper.

These books place readers in coaching situations where they must decide the best move. PA EA M *

• • • • • •

Survival

Alive, Paul Piers Reed. 1974.

This is an exciting true-life survival story about a group of soccer players whose plane crashed in the Andes. EA LA L

Dove, Robin Graham and L. T. Gill. 1972. Paper.

This journal of a sixteen-year-old who sailed his twenty-four-foot sloop around the world has fascinated many would-be adventurers. EA LA M

Land of the Snow Lion: An Adventure in Tibet, Elaine Brook. 1987.

This is a personal account of a trek through remote, off-limits areas of Asia.   EA LA F

Runaway, Lucy Irvine. 1987.

The author of *Castaway* (1984; paper) tells about her life prior to her self-imposed island exile.   EA LA F

The Snow Leopard, Peter Matthiessen. 1979. Paper.

An arduous trek through the Himalayas becomes a spiritual pilgrimage.   LA M

To Fight the Wild, Rod Ansell and Rachel Percy. 1986.

Stranded in Australia's Northern Territory after a boating accident, Ansell used his knowledge of bush lore to save himself.   PA EA M *

13

The Parents' Bookshelf:
Books and Magazines
about Adolescents

THE FERVENT PRAYER OF A
TEENAGER'S PARENT

Oh Higher Power,
And I wish I were—
Give me to know that the easier life is made
for the young, the harder they will make it
for themselves and each other.
Harden my heart and stop my ears against what
other people let their kids do.
Strike me dumb when I blame a teacher I have
never met, for heaven alone knows what that
teacher has heard about me.
Let not the coach build his career on the
vulnerable flesh of my son.
Spare my daughter the sly pornography of soap
operas.
Send summer reading lists so my children
won't lose three months of a fertile growing
season.
Sharpen my eye as I ransack my child's room
to find and destroy the fake ID.
Embolden my heart as I unplug the telephone

from my child's room so that the peer group
that rules the school all day will not rule
our nights as well.
Stay my hand when I am tempted to buy
children's love with credit cards in their
names, or mine.
Strengthen my spine as I impose a curfew,
lest my nights be a hell of waiting for the
fatal phone call.
And give me ears to hear when the young cry
out for new freedoms, they are demanding old
rules. Amen

Richard Peck

. . . . . .
Locating Material about Adolescents

Some of us dread our youngsters' becoming teenagers, remembering the difficulties of our adolescence. And some of us, as Louise Kaplan suggests, "have forgotten the painful emotions associated with becoming adult [and] tend to imagine the adolescent years as brimming with opportunity." Either way, we are likely to experience the difficulties of adolescence along with our children.

Unfortunately, help in dealing with adolescents is not easy to find. The number of books for parents of adolescents is a small fraction of those published for parents of infants. However, there are some books that can help us. The following books assist parents in understanding adolescents and suggest ways to make adolescence easier for parents and children.

Books for Parents

Active Learning: A Parent's Guide to Helping Your Teen Make the Grade in School, Peter D. Linn. 1993. Paper.

   A corporate trainer provides parents with practical suggestions for helping adolescents achieve academically. The ideas are simple, sensible, and likely to succeed.

Between Parent and Teenager, Haim Ginnott. 1969.

   Though a bit dated, this may be the most complete, helpful resource book for parents of teenagers. The book helps parents deal with conflicts with their young adult children and gives helpful examples throughout.   L

Books for You: A Booklist for Senior High Students (11th edition), edited by Shirley Wurth. Paper.

   This annotated booklist is meant to be used by students in grades seven through twelve. However, it is also useful for parents who are searching for appropriate books for their adolescents. The list is divided by topics, contains nearly eight hundred entries, and is updated every few years by the National Council of Teachers of English, from whom it must be ordered.

Boys and Sex (3rd edition), Wardell B. Pomeroy. 1992. Paper.

   This book for adolescent boys and their parents discusses the physiological, psychological, and social factors involved in the adolescent male's sexual development. The author stresses the importance of responsibility in healthy sexual maturing. A question-and-answer section addresses adolescents' common concerns.

Coping with Teenager Depression, Kathleen McCoy. 1985.

   This study of why depression is so widespread and destructive advises parents how to recognize depression and what to do about it.

The Essential AIDS Fact Book: No. 3 (3rd edition), Paul Harding Douglas and Laura Pinsky. 1991. Paper.

This is a frequently updated, easy-to-read source of information on AIDS and how to avoid it.

Experiencing Adolescents: A Sourcebook for Parents, Teachers, and Teens (revised edition), edited by Richard M. Lerner and Nancy L. Galambos. 1993.

The authors provide a guide to adolescent development and discuss what can be done to cope with the adolescent's problems.

Family Healing: Tales of Hope and Renewal from Family Therapy, Salvador Minuchin and Michael P. Nichols. 1992.

Among the anecdotal accounts here of how families with serious problems were able to mend is the story of the family of an adolescent drug addict.

Family Video Guide, Terry Catchpole and Catherine Catchpole. Paper.

This guide to all kinds of good family videos includes feature-length films.

Getting Your Kids to Say No in the '90s When You Said Yes in the '60s, Victor Strasburger. 1993. Paper.

Strasburger discusses the physical and psychological growth of the adolescent. He suggests ways that parents can help adolescents resist temptations such as alcohol, drugs, and tobacco.

Girls and Sex (3rd edition), Wardell B. Pomeroy. 1992. Paper.

This book for adolescent girls and their parents gives accurate information and practical advice about physical and emotional changes related to puberty. The author emphasizes the need for girls to have a comfortable understanding of their sexuality. A question-and-answer section deals with many common problems.

Great Videos for Kids: A Parent's Guide to Choosing the Best, Catherine Cella. 1992. Paper.

The book focuses on the home video market, recommending

many videos available at retail outlets. Library and feature-length videos are not included.

Hassle-Free Homework: A Six-Week Plan for Parents and Children to Take the Pain Out of Homework, Faith Clark and Cecil Clark. 1989. Paper.

This guide takes a step-by-step positive approach to helping children learn how to study and do homework. It includes organizational and motivational techniques.

Helping Your Depressed Child: A Reassuring Guide to Causes and Treatment of Childhood and Adolescent Depression, Lawrence Kern and Adrienne Lieberman. 1993. Paper.

This is a helpful book for parents attempting to understand and deal with adolescent depression.

High Interest–Easy Reading: A Booklist for Junior and Senior High School Students (6th edition), edited by William G. McBride. Paper.

This frequently updated booklist contains annotations of nearly four hundred books appropriate for adolescents with reading problems. The books are mature enough to interest adolescents and are easy to read. The annotated booklist must be ordered from the National Council of Teachers of English.

How to Help Children with Common Problems, Charles E. Schaefer and Howard Millman. 1989. Paper.

Parents are advised about dealing with problems of childhood and adolescence, including shyness, sex, obesity, and drugs.

How to Live with Your Teenager: A Survivor's Handbook for Parents, Peter H. Buntman and Eleanor M. Saris. 1990. Paper.

Teachers and parents are given specific steps to help adolescents deal with problems they may encounter.

The New Read-Aloud Handbook, Jim Trelease. 1989. Paper.

Appropriate for the family who wants to read and share books, this excellent guide contains extensive bibliographies of read-aloud books appropriate for all ages of readers and listeners.

Not My Kid: A Parent's Guide to Kids and Drugs, Beth Polson and
Miller Newton. 1985. Paper.

This is a practical guide to identifying a drug problem and
dealing with it.

*Read All About It! Great Read-Aloud Stories, Poems & Newspaper
Pieces for Preteens and Teens*, edited by Jim Trelease. 1993.
Paper.

An excellent source of great read-aloud stories appropriate for
adolescents, this collection contains motivating sections of
novels, interesting short stories, humorous and heartwarming
articles, and other enjoyable read-alouds. Also included are
biographical sketches of each author and information about
other books by the authors.

Surviving Your Adolescents, Thomas W. Phelan. 1992.

This book provides excellent, readable personal and professional advice on child management techniques, including setting up appointments to discuss problem behavior and taking
charge when there is no other alternative.

Talking with Your Child about Sex, Mary Steichen Calderon, M.D.,
and James W. Ramey. 1983. Paper.

Calderon, former president and cofounder of Sex Information
and Education Council of the United States, and Ramey, a be-
havioral scientist, help parents discuss sex and related issues
with children at different stages of development.

Teaching Your Children Values, Linda Eyre. 1993. Paper.

This is a simple to follow, sequential guide to helping children,
from preschool to early adolescence, develop values at home.

365 Outdoor Activities You Can Do with Your Child, Steve Bennett
and Ruth Bennett. 1993. Paper.

This book features many enjoyable games to get the whole
family out of the house and away from the television.

Travel Games for the Family, Marie Boatness. 1993. Paper.

This is an excellent guide to keep everyone contented in the car, on the train, or on the plane.

What Do You Really Want for Your Children?, Wayne Dyer. 1986. Paper.

This is a practical guide for raising healthy, happy, self-reliant, confident children.

Your Reading: A Booklist for Junior High and Middle School Students (9th edition), edited by Anne C. Webb. 1993. Paper.

Designed to be used by pre- and early adolescents, this is also an excellent annotated bibliography useful to parents attempting to find books appropriate for the maturity and interest levels of their adolescents. The book contains more than one thousand annotated book entries of titles published between 1988 and 1990. *Your Reading* is updated every few years by the National Council of Teachers of English, from whom it must be ordered.

Professional Books about Adolescence

Adolescence: The Farewell to Childhood, Louise J. Kaplan. 1985. Paper.

This academic but lyrical description of adolescence explores theories of adolescence and discusses the problems of modern teenagers, including independence versus authority, sexuality, growth spurts, mother-daughter relationships, and father-son relationships.

Boys Will Be Boys: Breaking the Link Between Masculinity and Violence, Myriam Miedzian. 1992.

This important book discusses how and why males become violent. The author suggests changes that need to take place at home and at school.

How Children Fail (revised edition), John Holt. 1988. Paper.

Though this book does not deal specifically with learning problems, it can help parents understand why their children have difficulty in school. Holt suggests many ways to help children learn to their full potential.

How Children Learn (revised edition), John Holt. 1988. Paper.

The author examines children's learning processes, grades and grading practices, testing, trust, and authority. He challenges the educational system and shows how parents can help their children learn.

My Mother/My Self, Nancy Friday. 1987. Paper.

In this fascinating narrative the author explores relationships between mothers and daughters.

A Piaget Primer: How a Child Thinks (revised edition), Dorothy S. Singer and Tracey A. Revenson. 1989.

This book examines the work and complex theories of developmental psychologist Jean Piaget, who many believe provided the most important insight into how thinking is developed. Though this book does not specifically address adolescence, it can help parents understand adolescents' intellectual development.

Young Girls: A Portrait of Adolescence, Gisela Konopka. 1983. Paper.

This sensitive presentation of an extensive research study on adolescent girls features comments from the girls in the study.

Magazines about Adolescence

The problem of finding current, helpful information about adolescence is probably most evident in magazines. Though there are several academic journals that deal with adolescence, there are no adult, mass-marketed journals devoted entirely to the adolescent. The following magazines offer a limited number of helpful articles in each issue.

Black Child Advocate. (National Black Child Development Institute, 1463 Rhode Island Avenue, NW, Washington, D.C. 20005)

This journal presents issues related to black children for professionals and parents.

The Exceptional Parent. (605 Commonwealth Avenue, Boston, Massachusetts 02215)

This magazine contains practical information for parents from preschoolers to early adolescents.

Gifted Child Quarterly. (National Association for Gifted Children, 1155 15th Street, NW, Suite 1002, Washington, D.C. 20005-2706)

This journal is designed to provide teachers and parents techniques for enhancing the education of gifted children of all ages.

Mothering. (P.O. Box 8410, Sante Fe, New Mexico 37504)

This magazine contains helpful information for mothers of preschoolers to early adolescents.

Parents Choice. (P.O. Box 185, Weban, Massachusetts 02186)

Reviews of children's media are provided to alert parents to trends and events in books, TV, records, films, and toys.

Parents. (P.O. Box 3051, Harlan, Iowa 51593-0015)

This magazine concentrates mostly on younger children but includes some articles on adolescent behavior and development.

The Single Parent. (Parents Without Partners, 7910 Woodmont Avenue, Washington, D.C. 20014)

Helpful hints about all aspects of parenting and family life are provided for single parents of children of all ages.

Working Mother. (McCall's *Working Mother*, P.O. Box 10601, Des Moines, Iowa 50336)

This magazine focuses on the needs of mothers who must balance responsibilities of work and parenting. It provides helpful suggestions for both worlds.

Professional Journals of Interest to Parents

Adolescence. (Libra publishers, 4901 Morena Boulevard, Suite 207, San Diego, California 92117-3425)

This scholarly journal with articles by physicians, psychologists, psychiatrists, sociologists, and educators contains many articles parents will find helpful.

ALAN Review. (Assembly on Literature for Adolescents–National Council of Teachers of English, 1111 Kenyon Road, Urbana, Illinois 61801)

This journal contains many reviews of new young adult book articles, as well as articles about the books and their authors.

The road to increased understanding is paved with books. Nearly every book written on adolescence begins with a statement about the difficulty of understanding adolescents. F. Philip Rice begins *The Adolescent* in this way:

> Contemporary Western society is ambivalent in its attitudes and feelings toward adolescents. Adolescents are admired, praised, and almost worshiped; they are criticized, belittled, and rejected.

We need books and articles to help us understand what is normal in adolescent development, to help us deal with the problems of adolescence, and to help us feel more adequate as parents of adolescents.

Sources

Atwell, Nancie. *In the Middle: Writing, Reading and Learning with Adolescents.* Boynton, Cook, Heinemann, 1987.

Beers, G. Kylene. "Choosing Not to Read: An Ethnographic Study of Seventh Grade Aliterate Readers." Unpublished doctoral dissertation, University of Houston, 1990.

Bettelheim, Bruno, and Karen Zelan. *On Learning to Read: the Child's Fascination with Meaning.* Knopf, 1982.

Carlsen, G. Robert. *Books and the Teenage Reader.* 2nd rev. ed. Harper & Row, 1980.

Chambers, Aiden. *Booktalk: Occasional Writing on Literature and Children.* Harper & Row, 1986.

Denham, Alice. "On Evaluating Teen-Oriented Periodicals." *ALAN Review* (Fall 1985): 13–15.

Early, Margaret. "Stages of Growth in Literary Appreciation." *English Journal* (March 1960): 161–67.

Educational Testing Service. *The Reading Report Card, 1971–1988: Trends from the Nation's Report Card.* Project of the National Center for Education Statistics, U.S. Department of Education. Princeton, N.J.: Author.

Ellis, W. Geiger. "To Tell the Truth or at Least a Little Nonfiction." *ALAN Review* (Winter 1987): 39–41.

Fader, Daniel, and E. B. McNeil. *Hooked on Books: Program and Proof.* Berkley, 1966.

Gallo, Donald R. "Are Kids Reading or Aren't They?" *ALAN Review* (Winter 1985): 46–50.

Gentile, Lance, and Merna McMillan. "Why Won't Teenagers Read?" *Journal of Reading* (May 1977): 649–54.

Hamilton, Harlan. "T.V. Tie-ins as a Bridge to Books." *Language Arts* (February 1976): 129–30.

Havighurst, Robert J. *Society and Education*. 8th ed. Allyn and Bacon, 1992.

Kaplan, Louise. *Adolescence: The Farewell to Childhood*. Simon & Schuster, 1985.

Kids Count Data Book: State Profiles of Child Well-Being. The Annie E. Casey Foundation, Center for the Study of Social Policy, 1993.

Kohlberg, Lawrence. *Essays on Moral Development: The Philosophy of Moral Development: Moral Stages and the Idea of Justice*. Vol. 1. Harper & Row, 1981.

Larrick, Nancy. *A Parent's Guide to Children's Reading*. 5th rev. ed. Doubleday, 1983.

Maslow, Abraham. *Motivation and Personality*. 2nd ed. Harper & Row, 1970.

Peck, Richard. "Some Thoughts on Adolescent Literature." *News from ALAN* (September–October 1975): 4–7.

Rice, F. Philip. *The Adolescent: Development, Relationships, and Culture*. 7th ed. Allyn & Bacon, 1992.

Rosenblatt, L. M. *Literature as Exploration*. 4th ed. Modern Language Association, 1983.

———. *The Reader, the Text, the Poem: The Transactional Theory of the Literary Work*. Southern Illinois University Press, 1978.

Scales, Pat. *Communicating through Young Adult Books*. Bantam.

Simons, Janet M., Belva Finlay, and Alice Young. *The Adolescent & Young Adult Fact Book*. Children's Defense Fund, 1991.

Spinelli, Jerry. "Before the Immaculate Cuticles." *ALAN Review* (Fall 1986): 15–18.

The State of America's Children, 1992. Children's Defense Fund, 1992.

Trelease, Jim. *The New Read-Aloud Handbook*. Penguin, 1989.

———, ed. *Read All About It! Great Read-Aloud Stories, Poems, & Newspaper Pieces for Preteens and Teens*. Penguin, 1993.

Tucillo, Diane P. "Getting Kids Hooked on Reading: What Public Librarians Can Do for Teachers." *ALAN Review* (Fall 1987): 15–16+.

Wells, Rosemary. "Books Remembered." *CBC Features* (January–June 1991).

The World Almanac and Book of Facts, 1993. Pharos Books, 1993, p. 196.

Zaharias, Jane Ann. "Fiction on a Floppy Disk." *ALAN Review* (Spring 1986): 58–62+.